GROTON PUBLIC LIBRARY
52 NEWTOWN
GROTON, CT 0634
P9-BYZ-491

THE *REAL* BENGHAZI STORY

OTHER WND BOOKS TITLES BY AARON KLEIN

SCHMOOZING WITH TERRORISTS

FROM HOLLYWOOD TO THE HOLY LAND, JIHADISTS REVEAL THEIR GLOBAL PLANS—TO A JEW!

THE LATE GREAT STATE OF ISRAEL

HOW ENEMIES WITHIN AND WITHOUT THREATEN THE JEWISH NATION'S SURVIVAL

OTHER WND BOOKS TITLES BY AARON KLEIN AND BRENDA J. ELLIOTT

IMPEACHABLE OFFENSES

THE CASE FOR REMOVING BARACK OBAMA FROM OFFICE

FOOL ME TWICE

OBAMA'S SHOCKING PLANS FOR THE NEXT FOUR YEARS EXPOSED

THE MANCHURIAN PRESIDENT

BARACK OBAMA'S TIES TO COMMUNISTS, SOCIALISTS AND OTHER ANTI-AMERICAN EXTREMISTS

THE *REAL* BENGHAZI STORY

WHAT THE WHITE HOUSE AND HILLARY DON'T WANT YOU TO KNOW

NEW YORK TIMES BESTSELLING AUTHOR

AARON KLEIN

THE *REAL* BENGHAZI STORY

Published by WND Books®, Washington, D.C. WND Books is a registered trademark of WorldNetDaily.com, Inc. ("WND")

Book designed by Mark Karis

WND Books are distributed to the trade by:
Midpoint Trade Books, 27 West 20th Street, Suite 1102, New York, New York 10011

WND Books are available at special discounts for bulk purchases.
WND Books also publishes books in electronic formats.
For more information call (541) 474-1776 or visit www.wndbooks.com.

Hardcover ISBN: 978-1-936488-86-5 eBook ISBN: 978-1-936488-87-2

Library of Congress Cataloging-in-Publication Data
Klein, Aaron.
The real Benghazi story : what the White House and Hillary don't want you to know / Aaron Klein.
pages cm
Includes bibliographical references and index.
ISBN 978-1-936488-86-5 (hardcover)
1. Benghazi Consulate Attack, Banghazi, Libya, 2012. 2. Benghazi Consulate Attack, Banghazi, Libya, 2012--Political aspects. 3. United States. Special Mission (Banghazi, Libya)--Security measures. 4. Diplomatic and consular service, American--Buildings--Security measures--Libya--Banghazi. 5. Terrorism investigation--Libya--Banghazi. 6. Stevens, John Christopher, -2012--Assassination. 7. Ambassadors--Libya--Banghazi--Death. 8. Embassy buildings--Security measures--United States. I. Title.
HV6433.L75K54 2014
363.32509612--dc23

2014013672

Printed in the United States of America
14 15 16 17 18 19 MPV 9 8 7 6 5 4 3 2 1

CONTENTS

INTRODUCTION

The most logical way to begin a book about the September 11, 2012, attacks in Benghazi, Libya, is to recount the timeline of the murderous assaults that targeted our U.S. special mission and nearby CIA annex. The Obama administration itself has provided a substantial portion of the publicly known version of events about that fateful night, and this outline was later re-crafted in more detail by a State Department–sanctioned review of the attacks. Key elements of the official chronology, however, have since been contradicted by Benghazi victims and witnesses, while particulars provided by the government have been denied by those who were on the ground inside the doomed facilities, calling into question the entire government narrative about what really transpired.

The White House should have lost all credibility on Benghazi after it was caught deceiving the American public by claiming the onslaught was the result of popular protests against an obscure anti-Islam film. Within five days of the attack, United Nations ambassador Susan Rice infamously appeared on five morning television programs (on Sunday, September 16, 2012) to push the "spontaneous protest" fiction, claiming the attack was in response to a "hateful video." Other Obama administration officials made similar claims. Four days after Rice's disinformation campaign, Obama himself described "natural protests that arose because of the outrage over the video."[1]

It would later emerge that the Obama administration knew from the beginning this was a well-coordinated, well-planned jihadist attack. The United States had surveillance video from the mission that showed no popular protest, while Gregory Hicks, the No. 2 U.S. official in Libya at the time of the September 11, 2012, attacks, testified that he knew immediately the attacks were terror strikes, not a protest turned violent. According to Hicks, "everybody in the mission" believed it was an act of terror "from the get-go."[2]

Numerous other whistle-blowers would later come forward with similar information. Even the CIA's Libya station chief sent an e-mail to superiors in the aftermath of the attacks, stating that the storming of the compound was "not an escalation of protests."[3]

Of course, we would need to suspend rationality to believe the administration's original claim of a "spontaneous protest." Tell me which spontaneous protesters would show up to the site with weapons, erect armed checkpoints surrounding the compound, and evidence insider knowledge of the facility, while deploying military-style tactics to storm an American mission? Which "spontaneous protesters" would know the exact location of a secretive CIA annex, including specific coordinates that were likely utilized to launch precision mortar strikes? Who even believes "spontaneous" protesters are capable of mounting a fierce, hours-long gun battle with U.S. forces stationed inside the annex?

The "spontaneous protest" claim is just the tip of the Benghazi misinformation iceberg. The State Department released an Accountability Review Board, or ARB, report that provided a timeline of the attacks, an accounting adopted by the Obama administration. The ARB is very specific about what it says happened that night. It claims the initial assault on the U.S. special mission in Benghazi started between 9:45 p.m. and 10:00 p.m. local time and lasted until about midnight, when all but two Americans were evacuated to the CIA annex about a mile away. According to the ARB, at midnight the annex was attacked intermittently for an hour by gunfire and RPGs. The next phase of the attack started at about 5:15 a.m. local time, the ARB claims, describing the second wave of attacks as consisting of heavy mortar and RPG assaults.[4]

However, witnesses on the ground, including CIA contractors who were inside the annex, said there was no lull in the fighting at all.[5] The "lull" claim was central to the Obama administration's explanation for why no air support or special forces were deployed to Benghazi. The White

House and State officials said they believed the attacks to have been over but were later taken by surprise by the continuation of the assaults. The new accounts cast a shadow of uncertainty not only over the timeline provided by the Obama administration but over every claim it made about Benghazi. If the administration lied about a "lull," how can anything else they told us about the assaults be trusted?

Benghazi witnesses further contradicted another central Obama administration claim. The State Department's ARB report specifically claims U.S. security personnel inside the compound were armed during the attacks, and the report even details how some security officers retrieved their weapons at the start of the assault. Witnesses, on the other hand, reportedly told a House Intelligence Subcommittee investigating the attacks that "none" of the security officers were armed.[6]

And so we see that we must question every aspect of the official narrative while attempting to divine the *real* Benghazi story. So much misinformation and disinformation is floating around about the Benghazi onslaught that to this day many in the mainstream news media continue to wrongly refer to the attacked facility as a "consulate," when it was something else entirely, as we will investigate.

I start this book by exploring the unprecedented "security" set up at the U.S. special mission. I will provide shocking new details about the withholding of critical protection at the facility while also investigating the mind-blowing decision to hire armed members of the al-Qaeda–

linked February 17 Martyrs Brigade as the official quick reaction force to "protect" the facility—essentially ushering the enemy inside the gates.

We will blow the lid off of the secretive activities transpiring inside the doomed facility, exposing a scheme to arm the jihadist Mideast rebels in what essentially amounts to the Fast and Furious gunrunning scandal of the Middle East, the Iran-Contra of the Obama administration. I will examine how these and other activities, including a separate weapons collection effort, may have been the motivating factor behind the September 11, 2012, assaults in the first place.

In one of the most devastating chapters, we will probe how a nonsensical decision made by Obama himself essentially sabotaged an operation in which Special Forces were just hours from capturing one of the most important terrorist figures charged with carrying out the Benghazi murders. An entire chapter is dedicated to investigating not only jihadist groups but also possible state actors behind the attack.

This book will shed new light on one of the persistent questions plaguing the Obama administration and its military command—why were no Special Forces or air support sent the night of the attacks? Not only will I offer new reasons for the lack of reinforcements, but we will also explore what our special forces were *really* doing the night of the assaults.

Of special interest are the details of what really happened to murdered ambassador Chris Stevens the night of the Benghazi attacks. The official State Department storyline regarding Stevens' fate has some glaring, but until now largely unchallenged inconsistencies. Again, this prompts questions about the official version of events. Foremost in our line of inquiry is whether at any point, alive or dead, Stevens was held hostage—and if so, by whom? I will show it is likely that the rebels were in control of Stevens' body at least for a period that disastrous night. If that was the case, how was the corpse eventually released? Were there negotiations to secure the remains? What promises did we make for Stevens' body, and to whom? If Stevens' body were held hostage, why do we not know about it? These details are important in comprehending the scope of the Real Benghazi Story.

Another crucial chapter explores the central role—really, roles—Hillary Clinton played in the Benghazi scandal, from her direct involvement in approving occupancy of the appallingly unsecured U.S. special mission, to the weapons-to-rebels scheme, to the very reason Ambassador Stevens was in the compound on the dangerous anniversary of 9/11. I will document Clinton's central role in virtually the entire Benghazi story, replete with information indicating she may have perjured herself during sworn testimony.

Yet another chapter is dedicated to the Real Benghazi talking points scandal. This sordid tale goes beyond the selective and misleading editing of intelligence information or the cover-ups of the well-coordinated jihadist assault. The implications of the duplicitous editing affair are larger than obscuring the possibly illicit activities taking place inside the U.S. special mission. The story here is the large-scale, purposeful deception of the American public, the abject betrayal of public trust to the point where national security was willingly jeopardized by stirring further riots across the Islamic world when the government decided to draw more attention to the Muhammad film, even misusing taxpayer dollars to apologize for the irrelevant movie.

The news media are also called out for their shady conduct in fostering misinformation, covering for the administration, and, with few notable exceptions, failing to do any real investigating even when the Obama administration's claims about what transpired made no logical sense.

In summary, I will explore how the Real Benghazi Story extends far beyond the deadly attacks on a U.S. special mission and CIA annex. We are today feeling the ramifications of the U.S.-coordinated arms shipments and vast supplies of aid and other support to the jihadist-led Mideast rebels, with conflicts being fueled from Syria to Egypt to Israel to Mali to Algeria. In fact, the Benghazi attacks may have ties to the 2013 Boston Marathon bombing and to the hijacking of an Algerian gas complex that targeted Westerners. In backing the rebels in Libya and later in Syria, the Obama administration may have helped create an al-Qaeda–allied army of thousands of highly motivated, well-trained gunmen. Besides wreaking havoc in the Middle East and Africa, these hard-line Islamists have been rampantly persecuting Middle Eastern and African Christians and other minorities. Among their ranks are Americans, Australians, and Europeans—jihadists who could return home to carry out domestic terrorist attacks. In each of these scenarios, the Benghazi scandals of 9/11/2012 are as yet unending. In these ongoing attacks on American allies and interests lie the ultimate answer to Secretary of State Clinton's now notorious question: "What difference at this point does it make?"

1

THE *REAL* "SECURITY" SITUATION AT U.S. SPECIAL MISSION

Let's start with the most basic understanding of what transpired in Benghazi, Libya, on September 11, 2012. If you ask most people to tell you what happened that fated night, a likely response will be that a U.S. "consulate" in Benghazi was attacked. For months after the dramatic events unfolded, the vast majority of all news media coverage worldwide referred to the U.S. facility initially assaulted as a "consulate," even though the government itself has been careful to call it a "mission" or "U.S. special mission." To this day, many in the news media continue to falsely report, perhaps out of sheer ignorance, that a "consulate" came under fire, while also informing the audience that a nearby "CIA annex" was the second target of the assault.

A *consulate* typically refers to the building that officially houses a *consul*, or an official representative of the government of one state located inside the territory of another.

Consulates at times function as junior embassies, providing services related to visas, passports, and citizen information. However, on August 26, 2012, about two weeks before he was killed, Ambassador Chris Stevens attended a ceremony marking the opening of consular services at the American embassy in Tripoli, meaning the functioning U.S. consulate was working out of Tripoli and not Benghazi.[1] The new U.S. consul in Libya, Jenny Cordell, was stationed at the embassy in Tripoli. A search of the State Department website finds no consulate listed in Benghazi.

Government documents from the State Department–sponsored Accountability Review Board (ARB) probe to congressional and senatorial investigations to documents released by the State Department, White House, Pentagon, and the U.S. Intelligence Community all carefully label the facility a "U.S. special mission" and not a "consulate." In fact, the ARB report divulges the mission was so special its classification "as a temporary, residential facility made allocation of resources for security and personnel more difficult."[2] The ARB report contains information that clearly contradicts any claim the special mission existed to serve as a liaison office to the local government, aka a consulate. It documents the local Libyan government did not know about the presence of the mission.

Even more stunning is a largely unreported revelation from the Senate's extensive, eighty-five-page report investigating the Benghazi attacks released in January 2014. The report, based on eyewitness and other governmental testimony, intelligence information, and thousands of classified and unclassified documents, related that key Pentagon officials had no idea there was a CIA annex that operated just 1.2 miles away from the Benghazi mission and was the second target on the night of the attacks.

> With respect to the role of DoD and AFRICOM in emergency evacuations and rescue operations in Benghazi, the Committee received conflicting information on the extent of the awareness within DoD of the Benghazi Annex. According to U.S. AFRICOM, neither the command nor its Commander [Gen. Carter Ham] were aware of an annex in Benghazi, Libya.[3]

The Senate was "puzzled as to how the military leadership expected to effectively respond and rescue Americans in the event of an emergency when it did not even know of the existence of one of the U.S. facilities."[4]

On the night of the attack, General Ham was placed in charge of the C-110, a forty-man special ops force maintained for rapid response to emergencies. The force exists for the very purpose of responding to events such as the Benghazi attacks. Command was transferred from the military's European command to General Ham's Africa Command in the middle of the attack. Ultimately, the C-110, which the military says was training in Croatia during the attack, was not deployed to respond in Benghazi. Instead the special ops were ordered to return to their forward operating base in Italy.[5] We will discuss this puzzling turn of events in far greater detail in chapter 3.

Regarding the CIA annex that was attacked, the Senate report reveals the facility was set up so that the movements of U.S. personnel were hidden from locals. The Senate report states that intelligence and State Department personnel should "generally be co-located overseas except where the IC [Intelligence Community] determines that, for operational reasons, co-location is not helpful in meeting mission objectives or that it poses a security risk." Keeping intelligence facilities separate from State Department compounds "can provide important operational advantages." The report quotes the unnamed chief of the CIA annex as saying, "We had the luxury that the Mission didn't have of keeping our compound low-profile and making our movements—we used very good . . . protocol movements, and our vehicular moves were very much low-profile." The annex chief continued: "So we had a security advantage, I guess you could say, over our State colleagues."[6]

The Senate report quoted a June 12, 2012, CIA cable from Benghazi, which said that as "a direct result of a concerted effort to build and maintain a low profile we believe that the locals for the most part do not know we are here and housed/officed in a separate stand alone facility from our USG [United States Government] counterparts." The report states that, according to the State Department, the nearby "Mission facility did not store classified information, and therefore no Marine contingent was present." [7]

BENGHAZI FACILITY "UNLIKE ANY OTHER IN RECENT HISTORY"

As far as security was concerned, the U.S. facility in Benghazi was one of a kind, according to the State Department's Libya desk officer, Brian Papanu. "Benghazi was definitely unique in almost every—I can't think of a mission similar to this ever, and definitely in recent history," he stated.[8]

Regarding the unusual nature of the U.S. facility in Benghazi, the House report stated: "Documents and testimony obtained by the Committee during the course of its investigation show that the *ad hoc* facility in Benghazi, rather than being an example of expeditionary diplomacy, was instead an expedient way to maintain a diplomatic presence in a dangerous place. The State Department was operating a temporary residential facility in a violent and unstable environment without adequate U.S. and host nation security support."[9]

Lee Lohman, executive director of the State Department's Near Eastern Affairs Bureau, testified that he couldn't remember U.S. diplomats ever having "gone into something in such an expeditionary way as this by ourselves without having military along with us."[10]

Indeed, because the facility was so dangerous and did not meet the security standards set by the State Department, the Benghazi mission actually required a special waiver in order to be occupied by American personnel, including Stevens. The Senate report notes that "although certain waivers of the standards could have been approved at a lower level, other departures, such as the co-location requirement, could only be approved by the Secretary of State."[11] Meaning Hillary Clinton herself provided regular waivers to ensure the continued legal operation of the Benghazi mission.

This information is staggering. We know from scores of reports and from details to be presented throughout this book that Benghazi staff repeatedly petitioned for more security. Yet Clinton provided waivers for the legal use of a facility that was woefully unprotected in one of the most dangerous hotspots in the world.

"YOU'RE ON YOUR OWN." NOT SET UP FOR PROTECTION

In a largely unreported item, a top State official revealed the State Department refused to install guard towers at the doomed U.S. facility in Benghazi, fearing the stations would draw too much attention to the compound. The admission by Patrick Kennedy, under secretary of state for management, raises immediate questions as to what was transpiring at the U.S. mission and why the State Department would fear drawing attention to the special facility.[12]

In an interview with CNN on November 18, 2013, Rep. Lynn Westmoreland (R-GA), chairman of the House Intelligence Subcommittee, disclosed that his committee had learned a directive was issued August 11—one month before the attack—telling Benghazi staff they were on their own. "And so we are looking into that directive to find out exactly who put that out," he stated. Westmoreland said the Benghazi compound "itself is not set up for protection." He stated that when his committee interviewed the people who were on the ground, "they said they were really surprised [at] the lack of security at the mission facility . . . [P]eople at the facility had been wanting help, requesting help, requesting additional security . . . [T]hey just couldn't believe that those guys were over there as unprepared and unequipped as they were."[13]

It tuns out the Benghazi facility may have violated the terms of the Vienna Convention on Diplomatic Relations, which governs the establishment of overseas missions. Like most nations, the United States is a signatory to the 1961 United Nations' convention. Article 2 of the convention makes clear that the host government must be informed about the establishment of any permanent foreign mission on its soil: "The establishment of diplomatic relations between States, and of permanent diplomatic missions, takes place by mutual consent."[14]

But according to the State Department's ARB report, there was a decision "to treat Benghazi as a temporary, residential facility," likely disqualifying the building from permanent mission status if the mission was indeed temporary. However, the same sentence in the report notes the host government was not notified about the Benghazi mission "even though it was also a full time office facility."[15]

Article 12 of the Vienna Convention dictates, "The sending State may not, without the prior express consent of the receiving State, establish offices forming part of the mission in localities other than those in which the mission itself is established."[16] If the Benghazi mission was a "full-time office facility," it may have violated Article 12 in that the mission most likely was an arm of the U.S. embassy in Tripoli, which served as the main U.S. mission to Libya, making the Benghazi facility an unauthorized mission.

ENEMY INSIDE THE GATES

If there were no guard towers, no military contingent, and the State Department all but refused to provide adequate security at the special mission, just who was protecting the compound?

According to the State Department, there were eight Americans present the night of September 11, 2012. Besides Stevens, there were two temporary-duty assistant regional security officers (ARSOs) who had accompanied the ambassador from Tripoli; information management officer (IMO) Sean Smith, who was said to have arrived in Benghazi one week earlier; and five diplomatic security agents, three of whom were assigned to Benghazi on short term.[17]

Due to the glaring lack of significant security at the mission and to the unarmed guards who served as the first layer of security, the State Department reached out to a UK-based security detail company that delivers security solutions for clients around the world. The mission's entire security therefore depended on "armed but poorly skilled Libyan February 17 Martyrs' Brigade militia members and unarmed, locally contracted Blue Mountain Libya guards," the State Department ARB report reveals.[18] Specifically, there were normally four armed February 17 Martyrs Brigade members who resided inside the compound's guest house building, acting as a de facto rapid response unit. In other words, these militia members worked within the gated complex. Blue Mountain, a private firm hired by the State Department, further provided five unarmed local Libyan guards "per eight-hour shift, 24/7, to open and close the gates, patrol the compound, and give warning in case of an attack," states the Accountability Review Board. The actual night of the attacks, only three of the four February 17 Martyrs Brigade members were present, with one militia man absent for several days purportedly due to a family illness.[19]

Now let's pause here briefly. Perhaps even more mystifying than the lack of significant security at the mission or the unarmed guards who served as the first layer of security was the presence of armed February 17 Martyrs Brigade members within the complex. Just who are the February 17 Martyrs Brigade?

The February 17 Martyrs Brigade is part of the al-Qaeda–linked Ansar al-Sharia, a militia that advocates the strict implementation of Islamic law and that took credit for attacks against other diplomatic posts in Benghazi before the September 11 attacks.

Ansar al-Sharia would become the first group to take responsibility for the Benghazi attacks in social media. The organization later claimed it "didn't participate [in the attack] as a sole entity," claiming the assault "was a spontaneous popular uprising" to an anti-Muhammad film that was released on YouTube.[20] Witnesses told the media they saw vehicles bearing Ansar al-Sharia's logo at the scene of the attack and said gunmen taking part boasted of belonging to the group. Some witnesses said they saw Ahmed Abu Khattala, a commander of Ansar al-Sharia, leading the attack.[21] Contacted by news media, Khattala denied he was at the scene.[22] In chapter 6 we will investigate how a strange move by President Obama all but thwarted a mission by U.S. Special Forces who were reportedly just hours away from capturing Khattala. More on that unreported scandal later.

Before you start asking why in the world the State Department would hire a known al-Qaeda–linked Islamic extremist organization to "protect" the special mission, consider this. Not only is this group part of the Ansar al-Sharia banner that reportedly attacked other Western outposts in Libya, but the February 17 Martyrs Brigade may have assailed the very mission it was hired to secure. That's right. The Senate's extensive report on the Benghazi attack reveals that the U.S. Benghazi mission "had been vandalized and attacked in the months prior to the September 11–12 attacks by some of the same [Libyan] guards who were there to protect it."[23] (It is unclear whether the guards referenced in the report were the February 17 Martyrs Brigade or the unarmed, local Libyan guards provided by Blue Mountain.)

LOOK WHO REFUSED TO HELP FLEEING AMERICANS

Did the al-Qaeda-linked February 17 Martyrs Brigade compromise U.S. security the night of the attacks? The Senate report for the first time reveals the February 17 Martyrs

Brigade militia refused to protect the U.S. security team that was trapped inside the compound. "Three armed members" of the brigade were present and working as part of the mission's security external detail during the attack. The security team asked brigade members to "'provide cover' for them to advance to the gate of the Temporary Mission Facility with gun trucks," the report says. "The 17th February Brigade members refused, saying they preferred to negotiate with the attackers instead."[24]

According to CIA notes, "the security team initiated their plan of assault on the mission compound" anyway. Some members of the brigade ended up getting into the vehicle, and a few members followed behind on foot to support the team.[25]

The Senate's picture of the February 17 Martyrs Brigade members refusing to "provide cover" contrasts sharply with the image of the brigade painted in the State Department's ARB report. The ARB report recounted the February 17 Martyrs Brigade complained to the local Libyan government on the U.S. special mission's behalf after a uniformed Libyan police officer was caught taking pictures of the compound before the attack. The ARB report states that as soon as the attack began, the Martyrs of 17 February Brigade guards advanced "towards the Villa B area." It also claims the brigade helped American personnel escape a roadblock while fleeing the compound. "The driver, ARSO 1, reversed direction to avoid a crowd farther down the street, then reverted back to the original easterly route toward the crowd after a man whom the DS (Diplomatic Service) agents believed to be with February 17 signaled them to do so."[26]

So were the February 17 Martyrs Brigade members helpful or not? It's hard to tell for sure, but according to the ARB report, the gunmen the night of the assault "appear to have used filled fuel cans that were stored next to new, uninstalled generators" to burn down one of the living quarters on the compound.[27] That's how the U.S. special mission was set ablaze. Did the February 17 Martyrs Brigade militia plan this? Were the fuel cans left there deliberately? Why aren't these glaringly obvious questions being asked?

As we will further explore in chapter 4, the intruders were said to have inside knowledge of the layout of the compound, including the precise location of a secret safe room where Stevens was later holed up. Was it the February 17 Martyrs Brigade that provided the attackers with that critical information? Were these militia members among the gunmen who carried out the actual assault that night?

I am not asking open-ended questions here. We will further explore the possible nature of the February 17 Martyrs Brigade's relationship with the mission in the next chapter, utilizing data to offer a plausible explanation for why these dangerous Islamist thugs were on the State's payroll and inside the gates of the compound.

SHOCKER: STATE PULLED AIRCRAFT, SPECIAL FORCES FROM BENGHAZI

Now let's put on steroids the question of why we hired

armed Islamic extremists to serve as our special mission's quick reaction force. The State Department normally provides security for our embassies and diplomatic personnel in the form of Security Support Teams (SSTs), which are made up of special U.S. forces trained for counterattacks on U.S. embassies. Reports have emerged that months before the September 11, 2012, assault, the State Department pulled the SSTs from the Benghazi mission.

It gets worse. In another largely unreported detail, the State Department denied a request for the continued use of an aircraft to move personnel and security equipment. Such an aircraft could have aided in the evacuation of the victims during the attack. Ultimately, the U.S. special mission had to wait for a Libyan C-130 transport cargo aircraft and other planes to be secured to move the victims from Benghazi to Tripoli and then from Tripoli to Western hospitals.

This bombshell information is contained in a February 2014 report by Republicans on the House Foreign Affairs Committee. The report documents that on May 3, 2012, four months before the attack, State Department under secretary Patrick Kennedy "terminated Embassy Tripoli's use of a DC-3 aircraft that provided logistical support to the SST."[28] We mentioned Kennedy earlier in this chapter for also denying guard towers to the mission.

According to *The Aviationist* blog, the Dos Wing DC-3 aircraft "provides a wide variety of missions, including reconnaissance and surveillance operations, command and control for counter-narcotics operations, interdiction operations, logistical support, Medical Evacuation (MEDEVAC), personnel and cargo movement by air."[29]

Shortly after the attacks on the Benghazi mission began, congressional staff met to discuss the events. In that meeting Lt. Col. Andrew Wood, a former Special Forces member from the Utah National Guard, "called the DC-3 'vital' to moving sensitive personnel and equipment to and from Benghazi and Tripoli."[30]

The State Department's ARB report into Benghazi doesn't once mention the cancellation of the DC-3 aircraft or the withdrawal of the SST forces. It does detail how evacuees, including victims of the attack, waited for several aircraft to be procured to aid in the evacuation of Benghazi following the attacks. The report notes that staff of the U.S. embassy in Tripoli, including the compound's nurse, took a chartered jet to help in Benghazi. That jet departed Benghazi with the wounded at 7:30 a.m. local time, or three hours after the final assault on the CIA annex in Benghazi. However, numerous other American personnel remained in Benghazi, apparently awaiting other aircraft.

The report states, "Embassy Tripoli worked with the Libyan government to have a Libyan Air Force C-130 take the remaining U.S. government personnel from Benghazi." The cargo jet did not arrive back in Tripoli until 11:30 a.m. The Defense Department sent two Air Force planes, a C-17 and a C-130, from Germany to Tripoli to evacuate the wounded. Those planes arrived in Tripoli at 7:15 p.m. local time, according to the Accountability Review Board.[31]

The detail about the State Department's cancellation of the DC-3 aircraft for the U.S. missions in Libya was first reported by CNN in October 2012, citing an internal State Department e-mail. At the time, CNN quoted State Department deputy spokesman Mark Toner saying it was common practice to use a DC-3 in locations where no commercial flights were available. "When commercial service was subsequently established (in Libya), we then moved that asset back to other State Department business," Toner added.[32]

However, unmentioned was that the DC-3 was recalled from Benghazi along with another Kennedy decision that makes little security sense. The House report relates Kennedy in July 2012 rejected the U.S. military's sixteen-member Security Support Team "despite compelling requests from personnel in Libya that the team be allowed to stay."[33] It was that SST that required use of the DC-3 aircraft.

Eric Allan Nordstrom, regional security officer at the U.S. Embassy in Tripoli, told House Republicans that "retaining the SST until other security resources became available was a 'primary issue' for him," the House report states. The House report did not find credibility in State Department claims that Ambassador Chris Stevens himself rejected the use of the SST. Gregory Hicks, the No. 2 at the facility under Stevens, "vehemently denied this claim," according to the House report.[34]

WHO'S LYING? BENGHAZI WITNESSES VS. STATE DEPT. ON "ARMED" GUARDS

As explained in the introduction to this book, it is difficult to recount the timeline of the attacks and the specifics of what transpired that night due to the conflicting reports from the State Department and the eyewitnesses. One of the many strange contradictions between the State-sponsored ARB version of events and testimony provided by Benghazi witnesses and victims regards whether personnel inside the U.S. special mission were armed during the attack.

U.S. Representative Westmoreland, chairman of the House Intelligence Subcommittee, told Fox News in November 2013 that State Department employees inside the mission were "not set up for any type of protection. When we interviewed these guys they said that they were really surprised at the lack of security at the mission facility." Westmoreland was commenting on closed-door testimony given to his intelligence committee.[35] He told *The Kelly File* on Fox News that none of the security officers were armed, and in fact, "one of 'em was barefooted, and I think they were totally unprepared for any type of attack."[36] Westmoreland was clearly referring to the U.S. assistant regional security officers (again, ARSOs or RSOs) who were inside the compound with Stevens during the initial assault.

Entirely unreported by the news media is that this witness testimony of unarmed personnel directly contradicts the narrative in the State Department's extensive ARB report, which specifically claims the personnel inside the compound were armed. The report states that the "ARSOs were each armed with their standard issue sidearm pistol; their 'kits,' generally consisting of body armor, radio and an M4 rifle, were in their bedroom/sleeping areas, in accord with Special Mission practice." It even claims that the officer who located Stevens "asked them to don body armor, and led them into the safe area in Villa C." He radioed in their location and then, "armed with an M4 rifle, shotgun and pistol, took up a defensive position inside the Villa C safe area, with line of sight to the safe area gate and out of view of potential intruders," the report notes.[37]

The ARB report describes in detail the process by which each security officer retrieved kits and guns:

> Following the SMC's emergency plan, ARSO 1 entered Villa C to secure the Ambassador and IMO in the safe area and to retrieve his kit; ARSOs 2, 3, and 4 moved to retrieve their kits, which were located in Villa B and the TOC. . . .
>
> From Villa C, ARSO 4 ran to his sleeping quarters in Villa B to retrieve his kit, while ARSOs 2 and 3 ran to the TOC, where ARSO 3 had last seen the Ambassador, and where ARSO 2's kit was located. (ARSO 2's sleeping quarters were in the TOC, making him the designated "TOC Officer" in their emergency react plan.) . . . At Villa B, ARSO 3 encountered ARSO 4, who was also arming and equipping himself, and the two then attempted to return to Villa C. They turned back, however, after seeing many armed intruders blocking the alley between Villas B and C.[38]

Remember Representative Westmoreland said the witness reported that the security officers were unarmed and one was barefoot. That would help explain why no officers reportedly fired any shots or even attempted to engage the intruders. Instead, the officers barricaded themselves in rooms. If that is accurate, does it mean the ARB report details were fabricated out of whole cloth? If those details were falsified, we cannot trust a word in the entire report. The ARB report claims officers did not want to engage the intruders because they were "outnumbered and outgunned by the armed intruders" so they "barricaded themselves in a back room" because they did not want to "compromise their location."[39]

WHAT'S THE WHITE HOUSE HIDING?

It is rare for Benghazi witnesses to speak out. The Senate's Benghazi report slams the White House, Pentagon, and especially the State Department for actively interfering in the investigation into the attacks. In a particularly stinging accusation that went largely unreported by news media, the Senate's extensive report by its Benghazi investigative committee charged a "strong case can be made that State engaged in retaliation against witnesses who were willing to speak with Congress."[40]

The lawmakers also accused the State Department of returning some witnesses to active duty so they were "shielded from, or actively avoided, Committee requests for interviews." The State Department treated these witnesses in an "unacceptable" fashion, and there is clearly no excuse for it.[41]

The Senate report revealed that not only have key executive branch witnesses declined to be interviewed, but the White House "still has not provided all relevant documents to the Committee." Other documents were only provided on a "read only" basis, meaning that the Senate committee was "only permitted to view them for a limited period of time, while being supervised by the coordinating agency," and they could only refer to their notes rather than the original documents when preparing their report.[42]

The Senate investigation noted the Department of Defense and other U.S. agencies provided hundreds of key documents, "although sometimes with a significant amount of resistance, especially from State. This lack of cooperation unnecessarily hampered the Committee's review."[43]

CNN reported that CIA operatives involved with the annex in Libya were being subjected to "frequent, even monthly polygraph examinations, according to a source with deep inside knowledge of the agency's workings." The goal of the questioning? To "find out if anyone is talking to the media or Congress," the source told CNN.[44]

The unusual manner in which the U.S. special mission was set up and the deliberate obfuscation (Pentagon members responsible for security in Africa were unaware of the *existence* of the annex), combined with information about an al-Qaeda–linked group providing "security," leaves us with one major question that trumps all others: What in the world was going on inside that ill-fated facility? The absolute lack of security seems to be very deliberate. The

State Department likely knew any major security presence at the compound would draw unwanted attention to the secretive activities taking place inside the doomed facility. It is the nature of those activities that we are going to explore in the next chapter.

2

"FAST AND FURIOUS" OF THE MIDDLE EAST

While most of the news media were still parroting claims of popular protests against our "consulate" sparked by an anti-Islam film, I received information from Middle Eastern security sources that told me otherwise. Twelve days after the Benghazi attacks, I reported that both the U.S. mission and the nearby CIA annex in Benghazi served as an intelligence and planning center for sending U.S. aid to rebels in the Middle East, with particular emphasis on shipping weapons to jihadists fighting the regime of Bashar al-Assad of Syria. Egyptian and other Middle Eastern sources also told me just after the attacks that Ambassador Chris Stevens himself played a central role in recruiting and vetting jihadists and coordinating arms shipments to the gunmen fighting Assad's regime in Syria.[1]

Prior to the establishment of the Libyan mission, the United States agents also provided aid to the rebels who eventually toppled Libya's Muammar Gaddafi. That aid, the sources stated, included weapons that were carefully purchased via extremist middlemen who used Arab and Turkish financing so as to avoid U.S. government accountability.

In this chapter, we will abandon statements from anonymous security sources and instead investigate documented information that strongly supports the contention that the attacked Benghazi facilities were utilized for these and other illicit activities in what might amount to the "Fast and Furious" of the Middle East, the "Iran–Contra affair" of the Obama administration. We will also examine how these activities, which seemingly included a separate weapons collection effort, may have been the motivating factor that prompted the September 11, 2012, assaults in the first place.

At immediate issue is the undeniable fact that a good deal of the anti-Assad rebels come from groups openly aligned with al-Qaeda, as well as a witches' brew of other anti-Western Islamic extremist organizations, including those declared official terrorist groups by the State Department. Another key issue is that until the end of April 2013, the White House had repeatedly denied it was involved in helping to arm the rebels.[2]

Besides White House denials, other top U.S. officials and former officials, including Hillary Clinton, have implied in congressional testimony that they didn't know about any U.S. role in procuring weapons for the rebels.[3] Central to the problem is the very notion of aiding extremist organizations whose stated goals include the annihilation of the United States, and worldwide supremacy for their brand of Islam. Their values are so backwardly antidemocratic; they are long known for persecuting Christians, Jews, the Druze, and other regional minorities, as well as secular Muslims.

FROM LIBYA TO SYRIA

Before getting to the Benghazi attacks, it is instrumental to briefly review United States–NATO military efforts from March to August 2011that helped topple Gaddafi's regime. Libya was supposed to be the lynchpin of the so-called Arab Spring, the well-intended blossoming of democracy, freedom, and human rights across the Arab world. It was around this time, in April 2011, that Stevens returned to Libya aboard a Greek cargo ship carrying "a dozen American diplomats and guards and enough vehicles and equipment to set up a diplomatic beachhead in the middle of an armed rebellion."[4] Stevens' original role in Libya was to serve as the main interlocutor between the Obama administration and the rebels based in Benghazi.

The news media churned out numerous reports of U.S.-coordinated arms being funneled to the anti-Gaddafi rebels starting at about the time Stevens arrived in Libya. In March 2011, Reuters exclusively reported that Obama had signed a secret order authorizing covert U.S. government support for the rebel forces in Libya seeking to oust Gaddafi.[5] Also that month, the UK-based *Independent* reported that "the Americans have asked Saudi Arabia if it can supply weapons to the rebels in Benghazi."[6]

In December 2012, the *New York Times* reported the Obama administration "secretly gave its blessing to arms shipments to Libyan rebels from Qatar [in 2011], but American officials later grew alarmed as evidence grew that Qatar was turning some of the weapons over to Islamic militants, according to United States officials and foreign diplomats." The article went on to say that the weapons and money from Qatar "strengthened militant groups in Libya, allowing them to become a destabilizing force since the fall of the Qaddafi government." The weapons came from Qatar and not the United States, according to the *Times*.[7]

While the Obama administration clearly was encouraging the arming of the rebels, the reports were careful to indicate that the weapons came from Qatar and not the United States.

At the same time we were reportedly arming the Libyan militias. Rebel leader Abdel-Hakim al-Hasidi admitted in an interview that a significant number of the Libyan rebels were al-Qaeda fighters, many of whom had fought U.S. troops in Iraq and Afghanistan. He insisted his fighters "are patriots and good Muslims, not terrorists," but he added that the "members of al-Qaeda are also good Muslims and are fighting against the invader."[8]

Adm. James Stavridis, NATO supreme commander for Europe, did not attempt to deny Libya's rebel force incorporated al-Qaeda. "We have seen flickers in the intelligence of potential al-Qaeda, Hezbollah," he testified to the U.S. Senate in March 2011.[9]

Meanwhile, numerous other mainstream media reports confirmed U.S. aid to the rebels fighting in Libya. Are we to believe that after the successful Libyan revolution and historic toppling of the country's longtime dictator, the United States closed up its guns-to-rebels program that turned the tide against Gaddafi just as the rebel-led insurgency against Syria's Bashar al-Assad was starting to heat up?

Indeed, our "Arab Spring" adventures pivoted westward when, according to the *New York Times*, the CIA started helping Arab governments and Turkey obtain and ship weapons to the rebels fighting the regime of Syrian president Bashar al-Assad. The *Times* reported on March 24, 2013, that this covert aid to the Syrian rebels started in early 2012. Syria began on a small scale and continued intermittently through the fall of 2012, expanding into a steady and much heavier flow later that year.[10] (My own sources say the airlifts started several months before the fall of 2012. I'll shortly present evidence of a massive arms shipment from Benghazi to the Syrian rebels in August 2012, one month before the Benghazi assaults.) Remember, this reportedly took place while the White House was publicly denying it had armed the Syrian rebels.

The *Times* reported that from offices at "secret locations," American intelligence officers "helped the Arab governments shop for weapons . . . and have vetted rebel commanders and groups to determine who should receive the weapons as they arrive." The CIA declined to comment to the *Times* on the shipments to Syria or its role in them.[11]

Where were these secret offices located? Could this be a reference to the secret CIA annex and obscure U.S. special mission in Benghazi, where Ambassador Stevens held his final meeting with a Turkish diplomat? Turkey, of course, was one of the main backers of the Syrian rebels.

The *New York Times* reported in December 2012 that Stevens himself facilitated an application to the State Department for the sale of weapons filed by one Marc Turi, whom the *Times* describes as an "American arms merchant who had sought to provide weapons to Libya." The *Times* reported Turi's first application was rejected in March 2011 but was approved two months later after he stated "only that he planned to ship arms worth more than $200 million to Qatar."[12] Qatar was Turkey's partner in aiding the Syrian rebels.

The *Times* does not question why Stevens would help facilitate Turkish government's application for an arms dealer. Nor did the *Times* bother to investigate the possible connection of these activities to the Benghazi attacks. After all, it doesn't take Sherlock Holmes to divine a possible link to the Benghazi assaults with a questionable weapons sale between a shady arms dealer and a U.S. ambassador in "secret locations" financed by Arab governments to be sent to Mid-East rebels, including some of the same groups linked to the September 11, 2012, attacks.

Interestingly, the *Times* reported U.S. intelligence officers aided Arab governments in obtaining weapons, "including a large procurement from Croatia."[13] In the previous chapter we noted the C-110 forty-man special ops force, maintained for emergencies like the Benghazi crisis, was reportedly "training" in Croatia during the Benghazi attacks. The force was not deployed to help the embattled Benghazi compounds. Given all the government distortions, lies, and cover-ups about Benghazi, it is certainly legitimate to ask whether the C-110 actually was being utilized to protect, collect, or ship the weapons reportedly procured from Croatia. We will further explore the curious story of the C-110 in chapter 3.

Let's get back to the *New York Times*' confirmation of arms shipments to the Syrian rebels during the period the Obama administration foursquare denied it was arming those rebels. The paper quoted a former American official as saying that David H. Petraeus, CIA director until November 2012, had been instrumental in helping set up an aviation network to fly the weapons to Syria. It further said Petraeus "had prodded various countries to work together" on the plan. Petraeus did not return multiple e-mails from the *Times* asking for comment.[14] In chapter 7, we will further explore the primary roles of Petraeus and Hillary Clinton in arming the Syrian rebels via a channel that included Stevens and others inside the Benghazi mission.

In March 2013, Sen. Lindsey Graham (R-SC) connected Stevens to an effort that involved weapons in Benghazi. He told Fox News that Stevens was in the Libyan city to keep weapons caches from falling into terrorist hands. Host Bret Baier asked Graham why Stevens was in the

Benghazi mission despite the many known security threats to the facility. Graham replied, "Because that's where the action was regarding the rising Islamic extremists who were trying to get their hands on weapons that are flowing freely in Libya." The senator stated, "We were desperately trying to control the anti-aircraft missiles, the man pads that were all over Libya, that are now all over the Mid-East."[15]

Previously, one source told Fox News that Stevens was in Benghazi the very night of the attacks "to negotiate a weapons transfer in an effort to get SA-7 missiles out of the hands of Libya-based extremists."[16]

In August 2013, CNN reported there is "speculation" on Capitol Hill that U.S. agencies operating in Benghazi "were secretly helping to move surface-to-air missiles out of Libya, through Turkey, and into the hands of Syrian rebels."[17]

As we will more thoroughly detail in chapter 3, there is good information that, aside from coordinating arms shipments to jihadists fighting in Syria, U.S. agents at the Benghazi mission were involved in an unprecedented multimillion-dollar U.S. effort to secure antiaircraft weapons in Libya after the fall of Gaddafi's regime.[18]

This weapons collection effort may go a long way toward explaining the motive behind the Benghazi attacks. The various jihadist organizations that looted Gaddafi's man-portable air-defense systems (MANPAD) reserves and the rebel groups that received weapons during the NATO campaign in Libya obviously would feel threatened by an American effort to try to retrieve those weapons.

FEBRUARY 17 MARTYRS BRIGADE

In the previous chapter, I asked why the United States would employ armed members of the February 17 Martyrs Brigade, a division of the al-Qaeda-linked Ansar al-Sharia terrorist organization, to provide "security" at the U.S. special mission? The exact nature of the Brigade's involvement with the mission might have been unintentionally exposed when a Libyan weapons dealer formerly from the February 17 Martyrs Brigade told Reuters in an in-person interview he had helped ship weapons from Benghazi to the rebels fighting in Syria. No one seems to have connected the dots from what the weapons dealer said to the activities taking place inside the Benghazi compound and whether the Brigade serves as a cutout to ship weapons.

In the Reuters interview published June 18, 2013, Libyan warlord Abdul Basit Haroun declared he is behind some of the biggest shipments of weapons from Libya to Syria. Most of the weapons were sent to Turkey, he said, where they were in turn smuggled into neighboring Syria. Haroun divulged that he sent a massive weapons shipment from the port in Benghazi in August 2012, days before the attack on the U.S. compound. The weapons were smuggled into Syria aboard a Libyan ship that landed in Turkey, purportedly to deliver humanitarian aid, he related.[19]

Ismail Salabi, a commander of the February 17 Brigade, told Reuters that Haroun was a member of the Brigade until he quit to form a brigade of his own. Haroun told Reuters his weapons smuggling operation was run with an associate, who helped him coordinate about a dozen people in Libyan cities collecting weapons for Syria. Let's pause here. This indicates Haroun, formerly of the February 17 Brigade, was possibly used as a proxy to ship weapons to Syria, and he may have also aided in the weapons collection effort.

Fox News may find one of its exclusive reports vindicated by Haroun's interview, information that may tie in to a motivation for the Benghazi assaults. In October 2012, Fox News reported the Libyan-flagged vessel *Al Entisar*, which means "The Victory," was received in the Turkish port of Iskenderun, thirty-five miles from the Syrian border, just five days before Stevens was killed. The shipment, disguised as humanitarian aid, was described as the largest consignment of weapons headed for Syria's rebels. Fox News reported the shipment "may have some link to the Sept. 11 terror attack on the U.S. Consulate in Benghazi."[20] That shipment seems to be the one described by Haroun in his Reuters article. Both Haroun and his associate spoke to the news agency about an August 2012 shipment with weapons hidden among about 460 metric tons of aid destined for Syrian refugees.[21]

A recent UN report appears to confirm that weapons were hidden in the *Al Entisar*, Reuters noted. A UN panel found that the loading port for the shipment was Benghazi, that the exporter was "a relief organization based in Benghazi," and that the consignee was the same Islamic foundation based in Turkey that Haroun told Reuters had helped with documentation.[22]

SECRET PRISON?

Besides weapons dealing and MANPAD collection, there have been some unsubstantiated reports claiming the CIA was running an interrogation center or secret prison at the Benghazi annex. A Fox News report quoted a well-placed Washington source confirming "there were Libyan militiamen being held at the CIA annex in Benghazi and that their presence was being looked at as a possible motive for the staged attack on the consulate and annex that night."[23]

Fox News further cited multiple intelligence sources who served in Benghazi as saying "there were more than just Libyan militia members who were held and interrogated by CIA contractors at the CIA annex in the days prior to the attack. Other prisoners from additional countries in Africa and the Middle East were brought to this location."

The same day Fox News originally reported on the alleged CIA prison in Benghazi, October 26, 2012, Paula Broadwell, the alleged mistress of ex-CIA director David Petraeus, gave a speech in which she claimed the CIA may have operated a secret detention center in Benghazi. The forty-one-minute speech, a keynote address at a University of Denver alumni symposium, was removed from the university's YouTube account after it was publicized in two links on the popular *Drudge Report* on November 11.[24] Following media inquiries, the video was reposted by the university at a different link. University of Denver spokeswoman Kim Divigil told me that day the video "was down for several hours this morning but immediately restored."

During the session, Broadwell stated, "Now, I don't know if a lot of you heard this, but the CIA annex had actually had taken a couple of Libya militia members prisoner. And they think that the attack on the consulate was an effort to try to get these prisoners back. So that's still being vetted."[25] It wasn't clear whether Broadwell was simply referring to the Fox News article about prisoners being held in Benghazi. A CIA spokesman flatly denied Broadwell's claim of a prison at the Libyan annex. He said the CIA "has not had detention authority since January 2009, when Executive Order 13491 was issued." Suggestion that the agency is "still in the detention business is uninformed and baseless," the spokesman added.[26]

Obviously Paula Broadwell is not exactly a credible source on Benghazi. However, her comments and the Fox News report simply add more to the mystery of the events surrounding the attack.

GOP'S INVESTIGATOR IGNORING REAL BENGHAZI SCANDAL?

One need not be a nuanced observer of international affairs to understand that any weapons collection or distribution program centered inside the Benghazi mission could be a critical detail in determining the main motivation for the jihadist assault against the compound. As noted in the previous chapter, such activities may also go a long way toward explaining why the Benghazi mission was established so secretively and why there was not a large U.S. security presence protecting the compound since such a visible security contingent would draw attention to the existence of the facility.

Yet Darrell Issa, chairman of the House Oversight Committee investigating the attacks, claimed in a radio interview that any involvement by the attacked U.S. Benghazi facility in arms trafficking "would have absolutely nothing to do with" the lack of adequate security at the compound where Stevens was murdered. Issa made the puzzling statement to radio host Hugh Hewitt after repeatedly deflecting questions about the alleged arms smuggling to al-Qaeda–linked Mid-East rebels based at the Benghazi compound.[27]

Issa claimed in the August 2013 radio interview that whether there was arms trafficking or not, it "would have absolutely nothing to do with whether or not you provide the security necessary for a long-time, loyal ambassador who was a specialist in the Middle East. I visited him in multiple Middle Eastern countries over his tenure. He was asking for more security. Asked about the reports of arms trafficking at the Benghazi compound, Issa told Hewitt, "It's not one of the items that we know, although I've seen it on the internet, too." Issa stressed his own investigation will only focus on why Stevens was denied sufficient security and why terrorists allegedly responsible for the attacks have still not been apprehended. (We'll discuss how Obama may have thwarted the capture of some of the most wanted Benghazi terrorists in chapter 6.)

When Hewitt asked Issa again about the reports of arms trafficking to the rebels, the congressman deflected the investigative task: "There's a specific [House Intelligence] committee chairman, Mike Rogers [R-MI], who deals with sources and methods and clandestine activities," Issa stated. "Our investigation really is about two questions. When you deny an ambassador security he needs, are you denying it because of gross incompetence, in which case nobody's been fired? You've got to ask why people aren't being held accountable. Or was this a political aim to make it look like the war on terror was over, that it had been won once Osama bin Laden had been killed?" Those are quite narrow investigative topics.

3

WHY NO SPECIAL FORCES OR AIR SUPPORT WERE SENT

One of the persistent questions plaguing the Obama administration and military command regarding the Benghazi episode is why no reinforcements were sent the night of the attacks. The government's standard response is patently absurd. They say they thought the attack was over after the initial assault, so therefore there was just not enough time to send a rescue mission or air support. But how could they have known what the gunmen had planned or that the first wave was the only attack to be carried out? Further, after the initial assault Ambassador Chris Stevens went missing. The acting assumption of the decision makers that night was that Stevens had been kidnapped, as documented in chapter 4. So why were Special Forces not immediately deployed for a potential hostage situation?

The controversy surrounding the decision not to send reinforcements should have been injected with steroids after

Martin Dempsey, chairman of the Joint Chiefs of Staff, made a bombshell admission during open congressional testimony. Dempsey conceded that highly trained Special Forces were stationed just a few hours away from Benghazi on the night of the attack but were not told to deploy to Libya

His shocking concession on available assets was broadcast live on C-SPAN, emitted in a room full of reporters. Yet his statements, which open a whole new line of questioning on Benghazi, have until this publication gone almost universally unreported by the news media, with the exception of my own coverage on my WABC radio show and in my WND.com and KleinOnline reportage. Like so many other aspects of the Benghazi story, Dempsey's remarks require the trained ear of a reporter familiar with the minutiae of the attack to fully comprehend the ramifications of what he said.

Dempsey made the statements in question during testimony before the Senate Budget Committee on June 12, 2013. The vast majority of news coverage of his testimony that day focused on his statement that U.S. Special Forces "weren't told to stand down" in response to the attack on the Benghazi mission. "A 'stand down' means don't do anything," he said. "They were told that the mission they were asked to perform was not in Benghazi, but was at Tripoli airport."[1]

While those quotes led most headlines on the Dempsey remarks, the words were not the most newsworthy comments made by Dempsey at the hearing. His admission of highly trained Special Forces near Benghazi is far more important. In comments that may warrant further investigation, Dempsey also stated that on the night of the attack, command of the Special Forces—known as C-110, or the EUCOM CIF—was transferred from the military's European command to AFRICOM, or the United States Africa Command. Dempsey did not state any reason for the strange transfer of command, nor could he provide a timeline for the transfer the night of the attack.

His remarks for the first time confirm an exclusive Fox News interview aired April 30 in which a special government operator, speaking on condition of anonymity, contradicted claims by the Obama administration and the State Department's ARB report that there wasn't enough time for military forces to deploy the night of the attack.

"I know for a fact that C-110, the EUCOM CIF, was doing a training exercise in . . . not in the region of North Africa, but in Europe," the special operator told Fox News' Adam Housley. "And they had the ability to act and to respond."[2] The operator told Fox News the C-110 forces were training in Croatia. The distance between Croatia's capital, Zagreb, and Benghazi is about 925 miles. Fox News reported the forces were stationed just three and a half hours away.

"We had the ability to load out, get on birds and fly there, at a minimum stage," the operator told Fox News. "C-110 had the ability to be there, in my opinion, in a matter of about four hours . . . four to six hours."

The C-110 is a forty-man special ops force maintained for rapid response to emergencies—in other words, they are trained for deployment for events like the Benghazi attack.

At the Senate hearing, Sen. Ron Johnson (R-WI) asked Dempsey about Housley's report. "The EUCOM CIF was not in Europe but actually deployed on a training exercise in Croatia. Is that correct?"

Dempsey confirmed, "It was on a training mission in Bosnia, right."

But Senator Johnson had asked if the forces were training in Croatia, *not* in Bosnia, and in later remarks, Dempsey said the forces were in Croatia. He neither explained the discrepancy nor even took note of it.[3]

Johnson then asked Dempsey if he agreed with Fox News that the C-110 could deploy in four to six hours.

"No, I would not agree to that timeline," he responded. "The travel time alone would have been more than that. And that's if they were sitting on the tarmac."

Dempsey's remarks are inaccurate. Even a large passenger jet can travel from the farthest point of Croatia to Benghazi in about two and a half hours or less. (Remember that in chapter 2 we speculated about what the C-110 may have been doing in Croatia, where there was reportedly a major procurement of weapons for transport to the Syrian rebels).

Dempsey further stated the command of the C-110, or the EUCOM CIF, was transferred the night of the attack, but he didn't explain why.

"There was a point at which the CIF was transitioned over to AFRICOM" from European command, he said. He could not give a timeline of when the command was transferred, telling Johnson he would take the question for the record.

Asked whether the C-110 left Croatia that night, Dempsey stated, "They were told to begin preparations to leave Croatia and to return to their normal operating base" in Germany.

Why was a special force that exists for the very purpose of an emergency like Benghazi told in the middle of a massive attack on our U.S. mission to return to their normal operating base instead of immediately deploying to Libya? Dempsey's statements confirmed the forces were not asked to deploy to Libya.

Why would the Pentagon deploy the C-110 to a training mission in Croatia during the anniversary of the September 11, 2001, terrorist atrocities—the one day jihadists worldwide are known to be the most motivated to carry out new attacks?

The C-110 Special Forces could have made a difference, according to the whistle-blower operator who spoke to Fox News. They would have been there before the second attack, he said. "They would have been there at a minimum to provide a quick reaction force that could facilitate their exfil out of the . . . problem situation. Nobody knew how it was going to develop. And you hear people and a whole bunch of advisers say, 'We wouldn't have sent them because the security was an unknown situation'."[4]

It is instructive to note that in his testimony, former deputy Libyan ambassador and whistle-blower Gregory Hicks said he contacted AFRICOM the night of the attack but received no support. Stated Hicks, "At about 10:45 or 11:00 we confer, and I asked the defense attache who had been talking about AFRICOM and with the joint staff, 'Is anything coming? Will they be sending us any help? Is there something out there?' And he answered that, the nearest help was in Aviano, the nearest—where there were fighter planes. He said that it would take two to three hours for them to get onsite, but that there also were no tankers available for them to refuel. And I said, 'Thank you very much,' and we went on with our work."[5]

Aviano, Italy, is 1,044 miles from Benghazi, about 100 miles farther than the Croatian capital.

Dempsey is not the only top military official to admit Special Forces were hours away. Gen. Carter Ham, the former head of U.S. forces in Africa, who had commanded those special forces after control was passed to him the night of the attack, confirmed the presence of the highly trained Special Forces. (Recall that Ham didn't even know about the existence of the Benghazi annex, according to the Senate's extensive 2014 investigation, as documented in chapter 1.)

Like Dempsey's comments, Ham's remarks were made in a public arena but were largely not covered by the news media. As I will show, Ham's explanation for why the military assets stationed abroad were not utilized during the attack raises more questions than it answers about his decision making. In remarks at the Aspen Security Forum on July 19, 2013, Ham stated he first received word of the Benghazi attack from his command post in Stuttgart, Germany.[6]

The EUCOM CIF "happened to be in Croatia at the time," Ham attested, "there on a six-hour notice, which is a pretty normal alert time." He further conceded that the force had "all their aircraft with them."

Asked why no outside forces were deployed to Benghazi during the attack, Ham responded that after the initial assault on the U.S. special mission, he believed the attack was finished. (This explanation, of course, has been contradicted by Benghazi witnesses, who described no lull in the fighting.)

Ham's explanation may raise questions about his stated judgment that night, which turned out to be mortally off base regardless of whether there was no lull in the fighting. Even if he believed the fighting to be over after the initial assault (a contention that within itself is highly questionable since he could not have known what else the attackers had planned, as noted earlier in this chapter), after the initial attack on the U.S. mission, there was a second round of deadly attacks against the nearby CIA annex, the location to which the victims of the first assaults were evacuated. And remember, even after the initial assault on the U.S. mission, Stevens was still missing, as Ham stated, so the deployment of a hostage rescue team may have been appropriate.

Asked why no forces were deployed to Benghazi after the initial assault, Ham told the Aspen Institute, "In my mind at that point, we were no longer in a response to an attack. We were in a recovery."

That statement appears to be contradicted by his next sentence.

"And frankly, I thought, we were in a potential hostage rescue situation, because the ambassador was unaccounted for," he said. So all the worst fears as a U.S. ambassador—being held hostage—were now being realized.

If he thought there was a hostage situation, wouldn't the deployment of Special Forces have been appropriate?

Ham stated that all they knew after the first assault "was that there was some kind of attack. "We knew from the embassy in Tripoli how many people and who they were," he said. "Pretty shortly thereafter we knew that the ambassador and Mr. [Sean] Smith were unaccounted for. But we didn't know much more than that."

Ham's further statements also prompt questions as to how he could believe the attack was over after the initial assault on the U.S. Benghazi mission. Ham admitted earlier in his remarks that he possessed no intelligence indicating any specific terrorist attacks were planned for Benghazi on the night of the 9/11 anniversary. Therefore, if he knew there was a clear intelligence failure, how could he have known whether the initial assault was a stand-alone attack or part of a multipronged attack, as it turned out to be?

CIA TOLD TO STAND DOWN?

U.S. government agencies, including the CIA, have long denied the persistent claim that there was a "stand down" order during the attack. However, CIA agents on the ground in Benghazi testified to lawmakers that they were loaded into vehicles and ready to aid the besieged U.S. special mission on September 11, 2012, but were told by superiors to "wait," a congressman privy to the testimony revealed. If accurate, this would contradict claims made by the State Department's ARB report, which states that the response team one mile away in the CIA annex was "not delayed by orders from superiors."[7]

Rep. Lynn Westmoreland (R-GA), head of the House intelligence subcommittee that interviewed the CIA employees, explained that while there was no "stand-down order," there was a disagreement at the nearby CIA annex about how quickly to respond. Westmoreland revealed that some CIA agents wanted to storm the Benghazi compound immediately, but they were told to wait while the agency collected intelligence on the ongoing attack.[8]

"Some CIA security contractors disagreed with their bosses and wanted to move more quickly," the Associated Press reported, drawing from Westmoreland's comments.[9]

According to AP writer Kimberly Dozier:

> Westmoreland said the CIA security contractors loaded into two vehicles, with weapons ready, the moment they heard the radio call for help from the diplomatic building. Some wanted to rush to the U.S. compound roughly a mile away, and their agitation grew as they heard increasing panic when the diplomats reported the militants were setting the compound on fire.
>
> The CIA team leader and the CIA chief at the Benghazi annex told committee members that they were trying to gather Libyan allies and intelligence before racing into the fray, worried that they might be sending their security team into an ambush with little or no backup.

> At least one of those security contractors, a former U.S. Army Ranger, was told to "wait" at least twice, and he argued with his security team leader, according to his testimony, related by Westmoreland. Westmoreland declined to share the names of the officers who testified because they are still CIA employees.[10]

The AP reported the CIA agents said a quicker response would not have saved the lives of those killed in the attacks, including Ambassador Stevens. That claim obviously cannot be verified because of the lack of information regarding what happened to Stevens the night of the attacks.

The narrative of "orders to wait" seems to directly contradict page 23 of the ARB report, which states:

> Just prior to receiving the TDY RSO's distress call shortly after 2142 local, the head of Annex security heard multiple explosions coming from the north in the direction of the SMC . . . The Annex response team departed its compound in two vehicles at approximately 2205 local. The departure of the Annex team was not delayed by orders from superiors; the team leader decided on his own to depart the Annex compound once it was apparent, despite a brief delay to permit their continuing efforts, that rapid support from local security elements was not forthcoming.[11]

In October 2012, CIA spokeswoman Jennifer Youngblood denied reports her agency was told to hold off in aiding those in the Benghazi compound. However, her statement only seems to pertain to her own agency and not others trying to help, such as U.S. Special Forces."We can say with confidence that the agency reacted quickly to aid our colleagues during that terrible evening in Benghazi," Youngblood said at the time. "Moreover, no one at any level in the CIA told anybody not to help those in need; claims to the contrary are simply inaccurate. In fact, it is important to remember how many lives were saved by courageous Americans who put their own safety at risk that night—and that some of those selfless Americans gave their lives in the effort to rescue their comrades."[12]

WHY NO BENGHAZI AIR SUPPORT?

There is much speculation as to why military assets were ultimately not sent. We can get creative and assert that the Obama administration didn't believe the attack would progress and so didn't want to draw more attention to a U.S. mission that was likely being used for sensitive intelligence purposes, like perhaps aiding the Islamic extremist–linked Mid-East rebels.

Another possibility, particularly for the question of why air support was never sent, may have been touched upon by a recent claim from an attorney representing Benghazi whistle-blowers. The claim may also help explain why it took hours for an American-provided C-130 cargo plane to take off from Tripoli for the short flight to Benghazi to help evacuate survivors, as documented in the State's ARB report.[13] I will present information that furthers the attorney's claim. In fact, these details may provide an explanation for why the U.S. Benghazi facilities were attacked in the first place.

Joseph diGenova, a former U.S. attorney who represents Benghazi whistle-blowers, stated that four hundred surface-to-air missiles were taken from Libya during the attacks and that the U.S. feared the missiles could be used to down aircraft. As you will shortly read, there may be a lot more to the missing antiaircraft story. Before we go there, let's review what DiGenova told WMAL radio in Washington, D.C., in August 2013. He said he "does not know whether [the missiles] were at the annex, but it is clear the annex was somehow involved in the distribution of those missiles."[14]

DiGenova said his information "comes from a former intelligence official who stayed in constant contact with people in the special ops and intelligence community."[15] He stated the Obama administration is worried the missiles can target airliners. "They are worried, specifically according to these sources, about an attempt to shoot down an airliner," he claimed.[16]

He continued: "And it's pretty clear that the biggest concern right now are 400 missiles which have been diverted in Libya and have gotten in the hands of some very ugly people."[17]

Obviously, antiaircraft missiles in the hands of the Libyan rebels or other jihadists would have served as a major threat to any incoming U.S. aircraft sent to aid the American targets during the Benghazi attack.

Such missiles also may have threatened the cargo plane that sat on the tarmac for hours in Tripoli before finally being dispatched in the early morning hours. The ARB report had stated that the plane took off only after security forces were able to secure the airport.[18]

In his testimony before the Armed Services Committee on June 26, 2013, Gen. Carter Ham was asked why no air support was sent to Benghazi. He replied that the military was facing a "very uncertain situation in an environment which we know we had an unknown surface-to-air threat with the proliferation particularly of shoulder-fired surface-to-air missiles, many of which remain unaccounted for."[19]

In House hearings, Maj. Gen. Darryl Roberson, vice director of operations for the Joint Chiefs of Staff, was further asked whether we provided rebels with any weapons systems, such as missiles, that could have been utilized against us during the attack. Roberson refused to deny that possibility. "Sir, I don't know that," was his response.[20]

The Senate's extensive Benghazi report documented the Pentagon was specifically concerned about MANPADS when military leaders discussed responding in Benghazi, explaining officials "worried about the presence of shoulder-fired Surface-to-Air missiles in Libya." The Senate committee spoke to outside experts who described a whole range of possible problems with dispatching aircraft, from MANPAD concerns to the lack of communication with friendly forces for marking targets. Still, the Senate determined more investigation was needed to "evaluate why DOD found it unnecessary to begin to prepare fighters and make other arrangements, especially in light of the concern that the hostilities could spread to Tripoli."

MANPADS PROMPTED BENGHAZI ATTACKS?

Amazingly, the story of missing missiles was first detailed in a largely unnoticed speech to a think tank seven months before the Benghazi attack. As I first exclusively reported, a top State Department official described an unprecedented multimillion-dollar U.S. effort to secure antiaircraft weapons in Libya after the fall of Muammar Gaddafi's regime. The official, Andrew J. Shapiro, assistant secretary of state for the Bureau of Political-Military Affairs, explained that U.S. experts were fully coordinating the collection efforts with the Libyan opposition. He said the efforts were taking place in Benghazi, where a leading U.S. expert was deployed. Shapiro conceded that the Western-backed rebels did not want to give up the weapons, particularly man-portable air-defense systems, or MANPADS, which were the focus of the weapons collection efforts.

The information may shed light on why the U.S. special mission in Benghazi was attacked September 11, 2012 in the first place. As documented in chapter 7, there is information the Benghazi mission was a planning headquarters for coordinating aid, including weapons distribution, to the jihadist-led rebels, according to informed Middle Eastern security officials. After the fall of Gaddafi, the arming efforts shifted focus to aiding the insurgency targeting Syrian president Bashar al-Assad's regime.

Middle Eastern security officials further stated that after Gaddafi's downfall, Stevens was heavily involved in the State Department effort to collect weapons from the Libyan rebels.

Those weapons were then transferred in part to the rebels fighting in Syria, the officials said.

Sen. Lindsey Graham (R-SC) last March disclosed in an interview with Fox News that Stevens was in Benghazi to keep weapons caches, particularly MANPADS, from falling into terrorist hands. Fox News host Bret Baier asked Graham why Stevens was in the Benghazi mission amid the many known security threats to the facility. Graham replied, "Because that's where the action was regarding the rising Islamic extremists who were trying to get their hands on weapons that are flowing freely in Libya."

The senator added, "We were desperately trying to control the anti-aircraft missiles, the man pads that were all over Libya, that are now all over the Mideast."[21]

BIGGEST MANPADS COLLECTION EFFORT IN U.S. HISTORY

Now, let's get to Shapiro's largely unnoticed remarks from February 2, 2012, which may shed further light on the activities taking place inside the attacked Benghazi facility. Let's recall the U.S. facility itself was protected by the February 17 Martyrs Brigade, which is part of the al-Qaeda–allied Ansar al-Sharia group. That group also was in possession of a significant quantity of MANPADS and was reluctant to give them up, Middle Eastern security officials previously told me.

In his speech seven months before the Benghazi attack, Shapiro stated, "Currently in Libya we are engaged in the most extensive effort to combat the proliferation of MANPADS in U.S. history." Shapiro was addressing a forum at the

Stimson Center, a nonprofit think tank that describes itself as seeking "pragmatic solutions for some of the most important peace and security challenges around the world."[22]

Shapiro explained that Libya had "accumulated the largest stockpile of MANPADS of any non-MANPADS producing country in the world." He also related how then secretary of state Hillary Clinton "committed to providing $40 million to assist Libya's efforts to secure and recover its weapons stockpiles." Of that funding, $3 million went to unspecified nongovernmental organizations that specialize in conventional weapons destruction and stockpile security.[23]

The NGOs and a U.S. team coordinated all efforts with Libya's Transitional National Council, or TNC, said Shapiro. The U.S. team was led by Mark Adams, a State Department expert from the MANPADS Task Force.[24]

Tellingly, Shapiro stated that Adams was deployed in August 2011, not to Tripoli where the U.S. maintained an embassy, but to Benghazi. The only official U.S. diplomatic presence in Benghazi consisted of the CIA annex and nearby U.S. facility that were the targets of the September 11, 2012, attack.

Shapiro expanded on the coordination with the TNC. "A fact often overlooked in our response to events in Libya, is that—unlike in Iraq and Afghanistan—we did not have tens of thousands of U.S. forces on the ground, nor did we control movement and access," he said. "This meant we did not have complete freedom of movement around the country. Our efforts on the ground therefore had to be carefully coordinated and fully supported by the TNC."[25]

Speaking of the missiles, Shapiro said, "Many of these weapons were taken by militias and anti-Qadhafi forces during the fighting." Later he explained that "because many militias believe MANPADS have some utility in ground combat, many militia groups remain reluctant to relinquish them."[26]

This prompts the obvious question for us—was the facility attacked by militias in an effort to thwart the collection of MANPADS?

Shapiro explained that the U.S. collection efforts consisted of three phases: "Phase I entailed an effort to rapidly survey, secure, and disable loose MANPADS across the country," he said. "To accomplish this, we immediately deployed our Quick Reaction Force, which are teams made up of civilian technical specialists."[27]

Phase 2 efforts were intended to help the Libyan government to integrate militias and veterans of the fighting, including consolidating weapons into secure facilities and assisting in the destruction of items that the Libyans deemed in excess of their security requirements.[28]

Such actions, we can imagine, were likely not supported by the jihadist rebels.

The third phase would have seen the United States help ensure that the Libyans met modern standards, including updating storage facilities, improving security, and implementing safety management practices.[29]

The U.S. efforts clearly failed in that phase. In April, the United Nations released a report revealing that weapons from Libya to extremists were proliferating at an "alarming rate," fueling conflicts in Mali, Syria, Gaza, and elsewhere.[30]

Meanwhile, what Shapiro failed to note is that he is somewhat complicit in the largest terrorist looting of MANPADS that took place immediately after the U.S.-NATO military campaign in 2011 that helped end Moammar Gaddafi's rule in Libya. Gaddafi had hoarded Africa's biggest known reserve of MANPADS, with his stock said to number between fifteen thousand and twenty thousand. Many of the missiles were stolen by militias fighting in Libya, including those backed by the United States in their anti-Gaddafi efforts.

CBS News correspondent Sharyl Attkisson later reported that the United States was unable to secure "thousands" of MANPADS. She quoted a "well-placed source" divulging that hundreds of missiles were tracked going to AQIM, a group in the Islamic Maghreb, which is the al-Qaeda franchise based in Algeria that is now considered one of the gravest threats to the United States.[31]

Could this missile threat explain why no air support was sent during the Benghazi attacks?

4

AMBASSADOR STEVENS KIDNAPPED?

Details about what really happened to murdered ambassador Chris Stevens the night of the Benghazi onslaught are sketchy to say the least. The official State Department story line regarding Stevens' fate has some glaring but, until now, largely unchallenged inconsistencies, to put it mildly. These inconsistencies prompt significant questions about the official version of events. Primary among our line of questioning is whether at any point, alive or dead, Stevens was held hostage, and if so by whom? I will show it is likely the rebels were in control of Stevens' body for a period of time that disastrous night. If this was the case, how was the corpse eventually released? Were there negotiations to secure the remains? What promises did we make for Stevens' body and to whom? If his body were held hostage, why do we not know about it? These details are important in comprehending the scope of the Real Benghazi Story.

Raising some eyebrows, Thomas Pickering, the State Department's lead Benghazi investigator and author of the State-sponsored Accountability Review Board report, refused to deny there was a plan to kidnap Stevens. At a House Oversight and Government Reform committee hearing on Benghazi in mid-September 2013, Rep. Cynthia Lummis (R-WY) asked Pickering directly about a potential kidnap plot.

"Is it true that they were planning to kidnap the ambassador and it went wrong?" she asked.

"I can't comment on that," Pickering replied, followed by a long pause.

Committee Chairman Darrell Issa stepped in and changed the subject. However, later in the hearing, Pickering further commented on the kidnapping issue. He stated: "Kidnapping seemed to me to be far-fetched. Because in effect in the testimony that was given and the public report, they did not make a serious attempt to go into the closed area of the villa. It is not even sure in my view that they knew the ambassador was there. So I would say, while I said I didn't want to touch that, I would say in retrospect it doesn't seem highly likely. It could be. But I don't think so."[1]

The kidnapping question was further fueled in part by an al-Qaeda member's claim that Stevens was killed in a botched capture attempt. Obviously we need to take anything a terrorist says with more than a grain of salt. But let's take a closer look at the jihadist's boast before we further probe the kidnap question.

Abdallah Dhu al-Bajadin, who was identified by U.S. officials speaking to the *Washington Free Beacon* as a known weapons experts for al-Qaeda, wrote on a jihadi website that Stevens was killed by lethal injection after plans to kidnap him during the Benghazi assault went awry. The *Free Beacon* reported al-Bajadin's claim was not immediately being rejected by U.S. law enforcement officials probing the ambassador's death.[2]

In the March 14, 2013, posting on the Ansar al-Mujahideen Network, an al-Qaeda–linked jihadi website, al-Bajadin claimed Stevens was given a lethal injection that was overlooked during the medical autopsy on his body. "The plan was based on abduction and exchange of high-level prisoners," he wrote; however, "the operation took another turn, for a reason God only knows, when one of the members of the jihadist cell improvised and followed Plan B."[3]

Al-Bajadin lectured that a lethal injection is given in "more than one place in the human body that autopsy doctors ignore when they see that the symptoms are similar to another specific and common illness. Anyone who studied the art of silent assassination that spies applied during the Cold War would easily identify these parts of the body," he said. The terrorist claimed he waited until the date of his posting to reveal the botched kidnapping and lethal injection because "the cell" behind "the infiltrative and secret operation is now completely safe from intelligence bureaus."[4]

OFFICIAL STEVENS ACCOUNT HIGHLY UNLIKELY

Let's put the al-Qaeda allegation aside and instead focus on the U.S. government's account of what happened to Stevens. We'd need to make several monumental leaps of faith if the official version of events surrounding Stevens' untimely death is to be believed. Here we must review what the State Department's ARB report on the Benghazi attack has to say about what it claims happened to him that doomed night.

Keep in mind this is the same credibility-challenged report that detailed that Stevens' guards retrieved their weapons and were fully armed during the attacks, particulars contradicted by Benghazi witnesses and compound staffers themselves, who claim none of the guards were armed during the attack, as we reported in chapter 1. Remember, since these details are relevant here, as you will see, this is the same ARB that may have given a faulty timeline of the attack, with witnesses claiming there was virtually no lull in the fighting.

Let's rewind to the beginning of the assault, when a diplomatic Security Service agent saw the armed men attempting to breach the compound and hit the alarm, shouting, "Attack! Attack!" over the loudspeaker.[5] Phone calls were reportedly immediately placed to the relevant U.S. agencies, including to a U.S. quick reaction force located at the nearby CIA annex.[6] Militants were said to enter the complex with cans of diesel fuel, setting the building ablaze and forcing those inside, including Stevens, to seek refuge in the bathroom until being overcome by smoke.

Diplomatic Security Service Special Agent Scott Strickland jumped out the bathroom window, but Stevens and Information Management Officer Sean Smith did not follow him, we are told.[7] Later, Strickland and three other agents returned to the main building to search for survivors, finding Smith's body, but not Stevens'.

The ARB details that Stevens' guard, identified in the State-sanctioned report not as Strickland but as "ARSO 1," located Stevens and Smith, "asked them to don body armor, and led them into the safe area in Villa C, which ARSO 1 secured."[8] An ARSO, as we discussed in previous chapters, is the State abbreviation for an assistant regional security officer.

Continued the ARB: "ARSO 1, armed with an M4 rifle, shotgun and pistol, took up a defensive position inside the Villa C safe area, with line of sight to the safe area gate and out of view of potential intruders. ARSO 1 gave his cell phone to the Ambassador, who began making calls to local contacts and Embassy Tripoli requesting assistance."

What the ARB claims happened next doesn't make much sense in light of other reports. The State document claims "ARSO 1, who was protecting Ambassador Stevens and IMO Smith in the safe area, heard intruders breaking through the Villa C front door. Men armed with AK rifles started to destroy the living room contents and then approached the safe area gate and started banging on it. ARSO 1 did not want to compromise their location in the safe area by engaging the intruders, and he warned the Ambassador and IMO Smith to prepare for the intruders to try to blast the safe area gate locks open. Instead the intruders departed, and the lights in Villa C appeared to dim."[9]

Now, why would the intruders simply depart before attempting to blast their way into the safe area? Earlier, the ARB itself noted the intruders appeared to have inside knowledge of the compound, a detail consistent with information documented in other chapters of this book. Fox News reported that the late Florida representative Bill Young said he spoke for ninety minutes with David Ubben, one of the security agents severely injured in the assault. Young said the agent revealed to him that the intruders knew the exact location of Stevens' safe room. "He (Ubben) emphasized the fact that it was a very, very military type of operation they had knowledge of almost everything in the compound," stated Young. "They knew where the gasoline was, they knew where the generators were, they knew where the safe room was, they knew more than they should have about that compound."[10]

Yet the ARB asks us to believe that just as these knowledgeable, well-coordinated intruders had Stevens cornered, they decided to leave Villa C, where the ambassador was holed up, without even attempting to gain entry to the safe room.

The story gets even weirder. The ARB report states that the intruders smoked up Villa C, likely to make breathing so difficult that anyone inside the safe room would need to come out. And that's just what happened: Stevens and his guards had no choice but to exit the safe room for fresh air. Except somehow Stevens and his guards made it from the safe room, where they were being smoked out, into a bathroom in the Villa without any of the intruders noticing? That's what the Accountability Review Board expects us to believe.

States their report ARB: "As smoke engulfed the Villa C safe area, ARSO 1 led Ambassador Stevens and IMO Smith into a bathroom with an exterior window. All three crawled into the bathroom, while the thick, black smoke made breathing difficult and reduced visibility to zero."[11]

"ARSO 1" escaped through a window, according to the ARB, believing Stevens and Smith were following him. He later reentered the building to search for Stevens and Smith. ARSO 1 made it to the roof of the compound, where he radioed for assistance. The report then relates that ARSO 1 was rescued by a small team that made it back to the nearby CIA safe house.[12]

From here, Stevens' fate gets even sketchier in the State report. During the attacks, ARSOs entered Villa C several times to search the building, finding and removing Smith's body but reportedly divining no sign of Stevens. That's it. No mention of the knowledge of the ambassador's whereabouts until approximately 0200 local time, when the Tripoli embassy was said to have received a phone call from ARSO 1's cell phone, and it was determined to have come from the Benghazi Medical Center, a detail that will become quite relevant for our purposes shortly.

The ARB claims a "male, Arabic-speaking caller said an unresponsive male who matched the physical description of the Ambassador was at a hospital. There was confusion over which hospital this might be, and the caller was unable to provide a picture of the Ambassador or give any other proof that he was with him. There was some concern that the call might be a ruse to lure American personnel into a trap. With the Benghazi Medical Center (BMC) believed to be dangerous for American personnel due to the possibility attackers were being treated there, a Libyan contact of the Special Mission was dispatched to the BMC and later confirmed the Ambassador's identity and that he was deceased."[13]

This description provokes several major questions. First and foremost: How in the world did Stevens' body get from a heavily besieged compound to the Benghazi Medical Center?

Here's the ARB's explanation: "BMC personnel would later report that at approximately 0115 local on September 12, an unidentified, unresponsive male foreigner—subsequently identified as Ambassador Stevens—was brought to the emergency room by six civilians. The identities of these civilians are unknown at the time of this report, but to the best knowledge of the Board these were 'good Samaritans' among the hordes of looters and bystanders who descended upon the special mission after the DS and Annex teams departed."[14]

In May 2014 an e-mail sent from senior adviser to United Nations Ambassador Susan Rice Eric Pelofsky to Susan Rice and other administration officials was released as part of the 112 pages of documents handed over to Judicial Watch to comply with a Freedom of Information Act lawsuit. The e-mail, which was sent on September 11, 2012, at 8:51 p.m. Eastern Time, or 2:51 a.m. Libyan time, in the immediate aftermath of the Benghazi attacks, states a phone call from a local Libyan hospital was placed by someone who reported Stevens was at the medical center and was "alive and well." The e-mail entirely contradicts the ARB report, which states the caller at the hospital said a man matching Stevens' description was brought to the medical center and was "unresponsive."

The e-mail was sent after the initial assault at the U.S. special mission and just prior to the second assault at the nearby CIA annex, according to administration timelines. It reads:

> Post received a call from a person using a RSO phone that Chris was given saying that the caller was with a person matching Chris's description at a hospital and that he was alive and well. . . . Of course, if he were alive and well one could ask why he didn't make the call himself.

Pelofsky could have been provided faulty information in the initial shock and confusion right after the attacks, but given the extent of the Obama administration's misinformation campaign surrounding Benghazi, we need to ask questions about this discrepancy regarding Stevens. Was the hospitalized ambassador "alive and well" or "unresponsive"? If Stevens was "alive and well" then how did he die?

"GOOD SAMARITANS"?

This "good Samaritans" claim makes little sense. The ARB itself documents the security officers fleeing the Benghazi compound to the CIA annex encountered heavy resistance on the way, including roadblocks set up by militants around the compound. The U.S. officers, the ARB relates, engaged in heavy fire clashes to make it past the compound periphery. Yet we are to believe that "good Samaritans" made it past those roadblocks with the body of the most high-profile American in Libya. And just who are these "good Samaritans" in Benghazi who risked their lives to make it through these checkpoints all the way to the hospital?

If you haven't seen the photos of Stevens' churned body being dragged through the streets, they certainly look real, although they haven't been verified. The gang of Middle Eastern men brandishing the ambassador's body definitely do not look like "good Samaritans."

The Stevens story gets stranger still. After we're told a "Libyan contact" went to the Benghazi Medical Center, a hospital the ARB calls "dangerous for American personnel,"[15] to confirm the presence of Stevens' body we hear nothing again about the American ambassador's corpse until later in the morning when a Libyan Air Force C-130 had been provided to transport the Benghazi victims to Tripoli.

All of the sudden, the ARB relates, "Annex personnel continued to reach out to Libyan contacts to coordinate the transport of the presumed remains of Ambassador Stevens to the airport. The body was brought to the airport in what appeared to be a local ambulance at 0825 local, and the TDY RSO verified Ambassador Stevens' identity."[16]

That's it. No explanation of how these "Libyan contacts"

managed to get Stevens' body out of the "dangerous" hospital.

Now, let's for a minute suspend independent thought and logic and assume the earlier ARB version of events is accurate: that "good Samaritans" indeed risked their lives to transport Stevens to the Benghazi Medical Center. A closer look at the hospital makes it seem unlikely the hospital staff simply gave up Stevens' body to the United States via Libyan contacts. The hospital, it turns out, was said to have been controlled by Ansar al-Sharia, the very group that was reportedly helping to lead the Benghazi attack. The center allegedly fell into the hands of the rebels during the U.S. and NATO–supported revolution that overthrew the regime of Muammar Gaddafi.

Enter Gregory Hicks, former deputy chief of the U.S. mission in Libya, the second in command in the country after Stevens. A detail provided in Hicks' congressional testimony may require further investigation in light of our line of questioning. Hicks said the U.S. embassy in Tripoli, Libya, was told Stevens was taken to a hospital controlled by Ansar al-Sharia, the group originally believed to have been behind the Benghazi attack.

Stated Hicks: "We began to hear also that the ambassador has been taken to a hospital. We don't know initially which hospital it is, but we—through David's reports we learned that it is in a hospital which is controlled by Ansar Sharia, the group that Twitter feeds had identified as leading the attack on the consulate."[17] Hicks was referring to David McFarland, the U.S. Tripoli embassy's political section chief.

At about three in the morning, Hicks received a call from the Libyan prime minister informing him of Stevens' death. "Before I got the call from the prime minister," he said, "we'd received several phone calls on the phone that had been with the ambassador saying that we know where the ambassador is, please, you can come get him.

"And our local staff engaged on those phone calls admirably," he added, "asking very, very good, outstanding, even open-ended questions about where was he, trying to discern whether he was alive, whether they even had the ambassador, whether that person was with the ambassador, send a picture, could we talk to the ambassador?"

He continued: "Because we knew separately from David that the ambassador was in a hospital that we believe was under Ansar Sharia's call, we—we suspected that we were being baited into a trap, and so we did not want to go send our people into an ambush. And we didn't."

Even more mystery was added to the quest for details on Stevens' death following the publication of a now-retracted book by Morgan Jones, who identified himself as one of the Blue Mountain private contractors who were hired to help train guards and provide external security at the Benghazi mission. The book by Jones, whose real name is said to be Dylan Davies, was recalled after it emerged that he reportedly provided contradictory statements not only to the FBI, but also in an unsigned Blue Mountain incident report said to have been his first-person account of what he did in Benghazi. Davies claimed in a *Daily Beast* interview that he was being smeared.[18]

We obviously cannot take anything Jones said as fact. My own personal review of his book leads me to believe that he seems to have inside knowledge of the inner security workings at the U.S. special mission, but there are legitimate questions regarding his true whereabouts during the actual attack.

The Blue Mountain incident report, which contradicts key elements of Davies' account in his book and in a subsequent *60 Minutes* interview, states Davies returned to his villa immediately after the attack. The incident report says Davies learned of Stevens' death from a Blue Mountain guard who had apparently secretly gone to the hospital and had taken a photo of the ambassador's body. Davies wrote in his book, however, that he was the guard who infiltrated the hospital and verified that Stevens was dead.[19]

Here's another discrepancy: The State Department's ARB report does not mention any other wounded American at the hospital with Stevens, but the Blue Mountain report goes on to claim a second American was at the hospital. "I asked [blank] if any other Americans were at the hospital and he said yes, a black man who had been shot in the hand. I presumed that this was one of the Ambassador's close protection team as both men were black." The report does not relate the fate of the other American it said was at the hospital.

The Blue Mountain report also contradicts statements by Ziad Abu Zeid, identified by the Associated Press as the doctor who treated Stevens at the Benghazi Medical Center. Zeid said Stevens was brought alone to the hospital and that no one at the facility knew who he was. The doctor told the AP that Stevens was close to death upon arrival at 1 a.m. local time, and "we tried to revive him for an hour and a half but with no success." Zeid said Stevens was bleeding from his stomach due to asphyxiation and did not have other injuries, contradicting Internet claims the ambassador's body was abused.[20]

Some of those abuse claims cite a Lebanese news outlet, Tayyar.org, that published a report falsely stating that Agence France-Press had reported Stevens was sodomized before being murdered. The AFP responded, issuing a statement that the Lebanese "report falsely quoted our news agency and has no truth whatsoever to it. AFP promptly sent a strongly worded complaint to that website and they removed the report and published a denial, saying that AFP did not report such a thing."[21] Even before the AFP denials, I personally found the rape rumors to be less than credible. Such activity is quite rare in jihadist circles.

UNITED STATES ASSUMED STEVENS KIDNAPPED

Enter the Senate's extensive, eighty-five-page report into the Benghazi attack. The report reveals a new detail about the assumption of Stevens' fate when he could not be found by U.S. security personnel inside the burning U.S. special mission. Reads the report: "State and CIA personnel re-entered the burning compound numerous times in an attempt to locate Ambassador Stevens, but to no avail. Under the impression that the Ambassador 'had already been taken from that compound and that he'd been kidnapped,' the leader of the Annex security team decided that U.S. personnel needed to evacuate to the Annex for their safety."[22]

So the U.S. security team inside the compound was acting under the assumption the Ambassador had been kidnapped. This was their official belief from approximately 11:10 p.m. local time until at least 2:30 a.m. local time, when it was reportedly established that Stevens was at the Benghazi Medical Center and was deceased. This means that for three hours the U.S. command and control were under the impression that gunmen were holding our ambassador hostage. It begs the obvious question as to why no special forces were told to deploy during those hours.

U.S. government e-mails released in May 2014 reveal a top Obama administration official was immediately concerned the entire Benghazi attack itself was a concerted effort to kidnap U.S. Stevens. The night of the attack, UN Ambassador Rice's senior advisor, Eric Pelofsky, sent an e-mail to Rice in which he expressed concern about a possible kidnap plot. "Yes—I'm very worried. In particular, that he is either dead or this was a concerted effort to kidnap him," wrote Pelofsky at 9:06 p.m. eastern time the night of the attack.

The Senate report for the first time reveals new details about "negotiations" to transport Stevens' body and how the corpse arrived at the tarmac with the waiting evacuation airplane. The report states:

> After more than three hours of negotiations and communications with Libyan officials who expressed concern about the security situation at the hospital, the Libyan government arranged for the Libyan Shield Militia to provide transportation and an armed escort from the airport. After learning that Ambassador Stevens was almost certainly dead and that the security situation at the hospital was uncertain, the team opted to go to the Annex to support the other U.S. personnel. The security team from Tripoli departed the airport for the Annex at approximately 4:30 a.m. Benghazi time. . . .
>
> Less than an hour later, a heavily-armed Libyan militia unit arrived to help evacuate the Annex of all U.S. personnel to the airport. The Ambassador's body, which had been secured by a local Libyan coordinating with the State Department, was also transported from the Benghazi Medical Center to the airport.[23]

Secured by a local Libyan? Just who was this "local Libyan" who secured Stevens' body inside an Ansar al-Sharia–controlled hospital? A medical center that was considered so dangerous that after three hours of negotiations the Libyan officials still didn't send in a militia out of concern for the security situation? Like so many other aspects of the official State Department story line, the claims about what happened to Stevens simply don't withstand scrutiny.

5

WHODUNIT?

The effort to determine which group or state actors carried out the September 11, 2012, attack is critical for many reasons, including divining the motivation for the assault and holding the appropriate party or parties fully accountable. We obviously must know whether these players are still motivated to act against us, while the United States will need to revaluate its current relationship with any country or party implicated in the assault.

In this chapter, I will investigate the various possible actors behind the attack. The most likely scenario involves the attack being carried out by elements of several Islamic militant groups, which begs the obvious questions: What was the common denominator? What would drive a witches' brew of jihadists, from al-Qaeda–linked groups to Egyptian, Libyan, and possibly even Yemeni and Algerian organizations to act in unison? Who organized the assault? Was blind hatred for the United States the main incentive, or was the attack an attempt to shut down specific activities transpiring inside the American facilities? If so, who stands to gain the most from the assault? Were these sordid jihadist groups being utilized by a larger player?

ANSAR AL-SHARIA

The first and most obvious suspect in the Benghazi attack is the al-Qaeda–allied Ansar al-Sharia militia operating in Libya. After all, the organization couldn't wait to first take responsibility for the attack in social media in the hours following the assault. The group later claimed it "didn't participate [in the attack] as a sole entity," stating the aggression "was a spontaneous popular uprising" in reaction to the anti-Muhammad film mentioned earlier.[1] As I reported in chapter 1, witnesses told the media they saw vehicles that bore Ansar al-Sharia's logo at the scene of the attack. They also said the gunmen taking part in the violence boasted of belonging to the group.[2]

Before we continue, I must briefly highlight the detail that armed members of the Libyan February 17 Martyrs Brigade, which acts under the banner of Ansar al-Sharia, were hired by the State Department to provide security at the mission while State denied other security measures, including its cancellation of the Security Support Teams of special forces trained for counterattacks on U.S. embassies. (This factoid was investigated in chapter 1.) The presence of the February 17 Martyrs Brigade clearly helps explain how the attackers reportedly had such intimate knowledge of the inside of the mission.

Ansar al-Sharia has now been fingered directly by the United States. In August 2013, the United States filed the first criminal charges in the attack, blaming a senior Ansar leader, Ahmed Abu Khattala. Some witnesses and U.S. authorities called Khattala a ringleader of the attacks. You will soon become more familiar with Khattala, whom witnesses placed at the scene during the initial assault on the U.S. special mission. The next chapter details the shocking story of how President Obama, whether wittingly or not, all but thwarted any possibility of capturing Khattala.[3]

Another Ansar al-Sharia leader charged with the Benghazi assault is former Guantánamo Bay detainee Abu Sufian bin Qumu, who reportedly heads Ansar in the Libyan city of Darnah. The *Washington Post* reported gunmen under Qumu's command participated in the attack, according to a U.S. official. Witnesses told American officials that Qumu's militia had arrived in Benghazi before the attack and that the information was used in part to designate Qumu's branch of Ansar al-Sharia as a terrorist group, along with two other al-Sharia branches.[4] Qumu, formerly a driver for Osama bin Laden, was released by the United States from Guantánamo Bay in 2007 and was transferred to a Libyan prison, where he remained until he was freed in a 2010 amnesty deal.

Incredibly, I found that one month before the September 11, 2012, attack, a fifty-four-page Library of Congress report that received almost no media attention warned that Qumu (which the report spelled Qhumu) was setting up shop in Libya and that his activities increasingly embodied al-Qaeda's presence in the country. The August 2012 report, prepared by the Federal Research Division of the Library of Congress under an interagency agreement with the Combating Terrorism Technical Support Office's Irregular Warfare Support Program, revealed that Qumu had a vendetta against the United States.

The document cited an Arabic interview in which Qumu was said to have "discoursed at length about his resentment of the United States, which he accused of torturing him during his Guantanamo detention, an experience that he said will not go away."[5]

According to the report, on June 7–8, 2012, a gathering of groups supporting Islamic law was openly held at Liberation Square in Benghazi. The event was hosted by Qumu's Ansar al-Sharia and reportedly was attended by members of at least fifteen militias, including al-Qaeda–affiliated organizations. The report further documented that al-Qaeda and affiliated organizations were establishing terrorist training camps and pushing Taliban-style Islamic law in Libya while the new, Western-backed Libyan government incorporated jihadists into its militias.[6] Despite this visible, growing al-Qaeda activity, including Qumu's noted presence and the establishment of terrorist training camps in the city, the U.S. facilities in Benghazi scandalously remained poorly protected.

At the time, Qumu was leading the al-Qaeda affiliate Ansar al-Sharia, which espouses anti-Western ideology. Qumu's group is particularly dangerous, the report warned, "as indicated by its active social-media propaganda, extremist discourse, and hatred of the West, especially the United States."[7]

The paper further noted that, because Qumu's views were so extreme, "Darnah's residents have accused [him] of carrying out attacks, especially targeting former Libyan officials but also people who disagree with al-Qaeda."[8]

EGYPTIAN MUSLIM BROTHERHOOD AND THE "BLIND SHEIKH"

As you will soon see, almost immediately following the Benghazi attack, the United States possessed information indicating some Egyptian participation in the assault, with links bringing us to the Muslim Brotherhood. Yet the Obama administration kept this critical piece of information from the public. Recall the attack took place fewer than thirty days before the November 2012 presidential election. Obama could have found himself in quite the political quandary if it were determined the Muslim Brotherhood had been involved in the Benghazi attack in any way. After the U.S. president called for the resignation of Egypt's longtime secular leader, Hosni Mubarak, Obama helped support the election of the Brotherhood's Mohamed Morsi and then infamously proceeded to open ties to Morsi's group.

Politics aside, the possible involvement of Egypt may be central in understanding what may have motivated some of the attackers and how the Benghazi assault could be linked to Morsi's campaign to free the so-called blind sheikh, Omar Abdel-Rahman, who is serving a life sentence in the United States for conspiracy in the 1993 World Trade Center bombing. Rahman's release has been a central foreign policy issue for Morsi.

In July 2013, several major Arabic newspapers ran a story, first reported by the Kuwaiti paper *Al Rai*, quoting a Libyan intelligence report on the Benghazi attack that mentions an alleged connection to Morsi and other prominent Egyptian figures. The report, prepared by Mahmoud Ibrahim Sharif, director of national security for Libya, was based on purported confessions of some of the jihadists arrested at the scene. It states that "among the more prominent figures whose names were mentioned by cell members during confessions were: Egyptian President Mohamed Morsi; preacher Safwat Hegazi; Saudi businessman Mansour Kadasa, owner of the satellite station Al-Nas; Egyptian Sheik Muhammad Hassan; former presidential candidate Hazim Salih Abu Ismail."[9]

Obviously, we cannot rely on Arabic media reports concerning claimed interrogations that likely were carried out under duress if they were carried out at all. Unsubstantiated Arabic-language reports from the Middle East also claimed a passport belonging to the alleged killer of Stevens had been recovered at the home of Egyptian Muslim Brotherhood deputy leader Khairat el-Shater. Senators John McCain (R-AZ) and Lindsey Graham (R-SC) reportedly visited el-Shater in prison in August 2013, spending over an hour talking to the Brotherhood leader.[10]

YouTube videos of the attack find some of the jihadists speaking a distinct Egyptian dialect of Arabic.[11] One of the videos shows a jihadist advancing on the U.S. special mission while stating in an Egyptian dialect, "Don't shoot, don't shoot, Dr. Morsi sent us."[12] There were also unconfirmed reports that Egypt would not allow the United States to interrogate suspects in the attack.

The original Obama administration claim of popular protests outside the U.S. Benghazi mission over an obscure, anti-Muhammad film might come back to haunt the White House in more ways than one. In perpetuating the now-discredited talking points about the film, the White House sought at first to connect the September 11, 2012, Benghazi attack to protests that same day in Cairo, Egypt, in which rioters climbed the walls of the U.S. embassy and tore down the American flag.

Those Cairo protests were widely reported to be acts of defiance against the anti-Muhammad movie. However, the protests were actually announced days in advance as part of a movement to free Rahman. In July 2012, Rahman's son, Abdallah Abdel Rahman, threatened to organize a protest at the U.S. embassy in Cairo and detain the employees inside.[13]

In fact, on the day of the September 11, 2012, protests in Cairo, CNN's Nic Robertson interviewed Rahman's son, who described the protest as being about freeing his father. No Muhammad film was mentioned. A big banner calling for Rahman's release can be seen as Robertson walked to the embassy protests.[14]

An Egyptian group was reportedly behind previous attacks targeting Western diplomats in post-Gaddafi Libya.

The State Department's ARB report on Benghazi itself noted that a jihadist group seeking the release of the blind sheikh, the Omar Abdurrahman group, made an unsubstantiated claim of responsibility for a June 6, 2012, bomb attack on the U.S. facility in Benghazi. The bomb exploded at the perimeter of the facility.[15]

There is information showing that murdered U.S. ambassador Chris Stevens or another U.S. employee was the target of the June 6 attack. The SITE monitoring group documented that the Rahman Brigades (the same organization the ARB report calls "the Omar Abdurrahman group") said they were "targeting a group of 'Christian overseers' who were preparing to receive one of the 'heads of instigation' from the State Department."[16] The group was calling for Rahman's release as well as vengeance for the death of Abu Yahya al-Libi, one of the most senior al-Qaeda operatives. Al-Libi, of Libyan descent, was killed by a U.S. drone in Pakistan in June 2012.

CNN previously cited a report that the Omar Abdel-Rahman Brigades was also responsible for a rocket attack against the convoy of the British ambassador in Benghazi on June 11 and an attack against the Red Cross in Misrata on June 12, 2012.[17] Further, the deadly January 2013 assault on an Algerian natural-gas plant was reportedly carried out as part of an attempt to trade hostages for the release of Rahman. Thirty-eight people were killed in a three-day siege that ended the hostage crisis. That assault may be linked to Benghazi, as we will investigate in chapter 10.

HILLARY'S BENGHAZI INVESTIGATOR CONFIRMS EGYPT LINK

In a development largely unreported by news media, the State Department's lead Benghazi investigator, Thomas Pickering, apparently leaked what was at the time classified information at a House hearing, revealing the government possessed evidence that an Egyptian organization was behind the Benghazi attack. Pickering of course was the author of the State Department's ARB report on Benghazi. His revelation begs the obvious question: Why was the government hiding information that an Egyptian group was involved in the attack?

At the aforementioned September 2013 House Oversight and Government Reform committee hearing on Benghazi, Rep. Cynthia Lummis (R-WY) asked Pickering, "Is it true that there's documentation that the Muslim Brotherhood and operatives from Egypt were involved in the attack?"

Pickering replied, "Our report indicates that one Egyptian organization which is named in the report was possibly involved. And I am not sure, I think that that's in the unclassified. I hope it is."[18]

The unclassified ARB report—which I know nearly by heart at this point—does not name any Egyptian organization as possibly being behind the September 11, 2012, Benghazi attack.

However, it would later emerge the group Pickering was most likely referring to was the Muhammad Jamal Network. In October 2013, the State Department declared the Jamal Network an official terrorist organization. Strangely, the official indictment of the group doesn't mention anything about Benghazi. The State Department's document only says, "Jamal formed the MJN after his release from Egyptian prison in 2011 and established several terrorist training camps in Egypt and Libya."[19]

In contrast to the State Department's designation, the Senate's eighty-five-page report on the Benghazi attack states there is information Jamal's Network participated in the assault.[20] Questions need to be immediately asked as to why in its indictment of the Jamal Network, the State Department does not mention that the group may have participated in the Benghazi assault, an act of war against the United States.

Even the United Nations fingers Jamal for Benghazi. A UN Security Council resolution from October 2013 added Jamal's Network to its list of sanctioned al-Qaeda groups. Unlike the State Department description, the UN resolution details Jamal's alleged involvement in the attack on the U.S. special mission and nearby CIA annex. A UN narrative summary of the sanctions resolution reads: "Muhammad Jamal set up a training camp in Libya where Libyan and foreign violent extremists were trained. Some of the attackers of the U.S. Mission in Benghazi on 11 September 2012 have been identified as associates of Muhammad Jamal, and some of the Benghazi attackers reportedly trained at MJN camps in Libya."[21] Those are pretty damning charges against the Jamal Network, yet the information somehow didn't make it to the State Department.

The *Daily Beast* confirmed an October 2012 *Wall Street Journal* report that fighters affiliated with Jamal's group participated in the Benghazi attack. The *Daily Beast*'s Eli Lake further quoted Seth Jones, associate director for the international security and defense policy center at the RAND Corporation, about Jamal's involvement. "There was at least one member and may have been more members from the Mohammed Jamal network on the compound for the attack on Benghazi along with members of Ansar al-Sharia and members of al Qaeda in the Islamic Maghreb," Jones stated.[22]

Guess who sprang Jamal Network leader Muhammad Jamal from Egyptian prison following the downfall of abandoned U.S. ally Mubarak? None other than militants from Morsi's Muslim Brotherhood. Also freed from prison during the Brotherhood-led revolution of 2011 was Mohammed al-Zawahiri, the brother of al-Qaeda leader Ayman al-Zawahiri. Mohammed al-Zawahiri was one of the backers of a protest at the U.S. embassy in Cairo, Egypt, the same day as the Benghazi attack.[23]

AQAP

Lost in the news media coverage about the Benghazi attack was that one day before the assaults, on September 10, 2012, al-Qaeda leader Ayman al-Zawahiri released a video on a jihadi online forum, calling for jihadists, and particularly those in Libya, to mount attacks against Americans in Libya, to avenge the death of Abu Yahya al-Libi. As noted earlier in this chapter, al-Libi, a senior al-Qaeda operative, was killed by a U.S. drone strike. "His blood urges you and incites you to fight and kill the crusaders," al-Zawahiri said. The forty-two-minute video was released fewer than eighteen hours before the Benghazi attack.[24]

In May, CNN quoted sources disclosing several Yemeni men belonging to Al-Qaeda in the Arabian Peninsula, or AQAP, took part in the Benghazi attacks.[25] AQAP, primarily active in Yemen and Saudi Arabia, is considered one of the deadliest members of the al-Qaeda franchise.

One senior U.S. law enforcement official told CNN that "three or four members of al-Qaeda in the Arabian Peninsula" took part in the attack. Another source quoted by CNN as being briefed on the Benghazi investigation said Western intelligence services "suspect the men may have been sent by the group specifically to carry out the attack.

"But it's not been ruled out that they were already in the city and participated as the opportunity arose," continued the CNN report. In chapter 10, we will trace those AQAP members to Algeria, Mali, and beyond and probe the involvement of various groups tied to other recent anti-Western attacks.

IRANIAN INVOLVEMENT?

Now that we see the most likely scenario involves a panoply of jihadist groups participating in the attack, the obvious question becomes why they were acting in unison. What common thread runs through all these groups? Certainly each one is friendly toward the cause of al-Qaeda and creating an Islamic caliphate. But why attack the obscure U.S. mission? Of course, there is the strong possibility, explored at length in this book, that these organizations were acting to thwart the alleged weapons collection effort headquartered inside the U.S. Benghazi mission. (We allegedly provided weapons to the Mid-East rebels and now were purportedly collecting those weapons, plus missiles looted from Gaddafi. Some of the weapons may have been passed to rebels in Syria.) This would certainly be a major motivator. Jihadist groups throughout Libya and beyond were directly threatened by the U.S. weapons collection campaign.

Some have posited Iranian involvement in the Benghazi attack. While I have found no concrete evidence supporting this link, the theory is quite interesting and does make sense. Iranian involvement could help explain why the mission and nearby CIA annex had been targeted. If the mission were aiding Mid-East rebels in Syria, as we documented, what would al-Qaeda and its affiliates stand to gain from organizing an attack against the very headquarters that was their pipeline for more weapons to be sent to Syria? Al-Qaeda was looking to oust Syrian president Bashar al-Assad.

One detail that always stood out for me was the apparent lack of a centralized al-Qaeda involvement in the Benghazi attack. Instead, it seems we are talking about local al-Qaeda–linked militias. Some of the groups may have even parted ways from the central al-Qaeda franchise. Khattala, for example, was said to have been displeased with some rebel groups, accusing them of abandoning Islamic doctrine.[26] Were these ragtag organizations operating under the patronage of a state sponsor like Iran that absolutely would stand to gain from assaulting the compound that was allegedly so central to the effort of toppling Iran's main ally, Syrian's Assad?

Iran's use of scores of local militias from different countries would serve as a brilliant smoke screen to obscure its own criminal involvement. While we are busy tracing the various participating groups to Mali, Egypt, and beyond, it could be these organizations were subsets of larger al-Qaeda–linked groups acting, wittingly or not, as hired guns for Iran. The Iranians certainly have a long and sordid history of state sponsorship of Sunni Muslim terror organizations, including Hamas, the Palestinian Islamic Jihad, and the Popular Resistance Committees.

In what may be a coincidence, it just so happens that former Hillary Clinton deputy chief of staff Jake Sullivan reportedly "secretly jetted to the Middle Eastern nation of Oman" to meet with Iranian officials as part of backdoor talks to broker a nuclear agreement with Tehran.[27] Sullivan was also Hillary's point man in helping to craft the now-discredited White House talking points on Benghazi.[28] Some on the Internet have been using that link to finger Iran in Benghazi.

Larry Johnson, a former CIA worker and former employee of the State Department's Office of Counter Terrorism, asked whether Iran was behind the Benghazi attack. He wrote: "Iran, who supports Syria's Assad, has a very effective intelligence organization. Once they learned that Libya was supplying fighters in Syria, do you think there is any chance that they (the Iranians) would want to shutdown that operation?"[29]

Johnson further questioned:

> 1. Did Iran infiltrate the fighters being trained by the United States and, in the process, gather intel that they subsequently used to target both the "Consulate" and the CIA Annex?
>
> 2. Did Iran prepare a cover for action and plant information on Facebook and other social media sites claiming credit for the attack in the name of Ansar Al Sharia?"

Writing at *Israel National News*, Mark Langfan surmises "Benghazi leads to Iran, not al Qaeda." Without citing evidence, Langfan says Obama is "doing everything in the universe to shut the Benghazi investigation" because "the truth of the Benghazi gun-running operation immediately leads to the likely conclusion that Iran, and only Iran, had the motive to attack our Benghazi consulate and murder Ambassador Stevens."[30]

Freelance journalist Marinka Peschmann wrote that a "Benghazi whistleblower source" told her "the immediate concern for the Obama-Clinton regime after the attack in Benghazi was to cover up the connection with Iran and Syria to Ansar al Sharia and Al-Qaeda in the Islamic Maghreb (AQIM)."[31]

Was Iran indeed involved? We cannot dismiss that as a possibility. While I have not yet seen any credible evidence, the notion is certainly logical. At this point all we can do is continue to ask questions and analyze the new information as it becomes available. Perhaps some of that information will lead us to the mullahs in Tehran.

6

THE *REAL* REASON BENGHAZI SUSPECTS NOT CAPTURED

Not only has the White House obfuscated legislative investigations into the September 11, 2012, Benghazi attack. And not only have key officials been caught misinforming the public about the events of that night. In one of the most mind-blowing moves of all, Obama himself essentially sabotaged an operation in which Special Forces were just hours from capturing one of the most important terrorist figures charged with carrying out the Benghazi murders. Even CNN, the *Washington Post*, and top U.S. officials are asking uncomfortable questions in a case that has rendered it nearly impossible for our forces to capture the militant. The odd case requires a journey into a split-screen, real-life movie unfolding on two separate fronts in Libya.

Questions need to be raised about the timing and manner in which the United States in October 2013 seized wanted militant Abu Anas al-Libi, who was living openly in his home in Libya and likely could have been captured at a different time.

(Anas al-Libi is not to be confused with al-Qaeda leader Abu Yahya al-Libi, who was killed by a U.S. drone strike in 2012. I myself have been confused at times with similar terrorist names. Some may recall the time WABC Radio's John Batchelor and I called the wrong terrorist during an on-air interview and proceeded to grill said terrorist for an attack that his group took no part in, mistaking him for another jihadist with a similar name, whose phone number had been stored in my cell phone the same way. Batchelor and I did not realize what happened until after our interview with one very confused terrorist had ended.)

It is now becoming increasingly clear the decision to capture al-Libi all but thwarted an ongoing operation in which covert U.S. operatives were tracking the every move of Ahmed Abu Khattala, a senior leader of the Ansar al-Sharia militia wanted for the Benghazi attack. The operatives were on standby, ready to seize Khattala, waiting for orders to carry out the most significant seizure of a suspect charged with the Benghazi attack. The Libyan government reportedly granted the United States permission to seize both al-Libi and Khattala. Due to al-Libi's capture, the Libyan government has clamped down on any further U.S. raids, making it astronomically difficult to go after Benghazi suspects.

Let's start with Khattala. In August 2013, almost one year after the assault, the United States filed the first criminal charges in the attack. Khattala, whom witnesses placed at the scene during the initial assault on the U.S. special mission, was reportedly charged under seal, meaning the details of the accusations are unknown. The FBI and Justice Department refused to comment to CNN, which first reported on the charges.[1] Some witnesses and U.S. authorities called Khattala a ringleader of the attacks.[2] We discussed in previous chapters that Khattala's al-Qaeda–linked Ansar al-Sharia group advocates strict Sharia implementation and the creation of the Islamic caliphate. The group infamously first took credit for the attack in social media, while later claiming it "didn't participate [in the attack] as a sole entity."[3] Witnesses told the media that not only did they see Ansar al-Sharia men laying siege to the compound; they also spotted vehicles brandishing Ansar al-Sharia's logo at the scene.

Khattala went somewhat underground after charges were filed in the United States. Still, prior to and in the days following the filings, he gave several interviews to the international news media in which he praised the attacks but denied personal responsibility. Speaking to the *New York Times*, Khattala hailed his Ansar al-Sharia organization as "good people with good goals, which are trying to implement Islamic law," and who are "bigger than a brigade [. . .] It is a movement."[4]

Now let's take a closer look at Anas al-Libi. He was fingered for allegedly helping to plan the 1998 U.S. embassy bombings in the East African cities of Dar es Salaam and Nairobi. The indictment accuses al-Libi, a computer expert for al-Qaeda, of personally carrying out surveillance of potential U.S., British, French, and Israeli targets in Nairobi for possible attack by al-Qaeda and the Egyptian Islamic Jihad.[5] Like Khattala, al-Libi gave scores of interviews to the international news media, including some from his home.

Al-Libi was seized in a very public operation in Tripoli by U.S. Special Forces on October 5 in a daylight raid outside his home while his family looked on. Family members immediately and predictably told the news media about the raid. The Associated Press quoted al-Libi's family saying that foreign-looking agents in a three-car convoy seized al-Libi while they watched. Al-Libi's brother, Nabih, told the AP he was parking his car outside his house after dawn prayers when the gunmen in the convoy encircled his vehicle and seized his gun before grabbing al-Libi. Nabih also told the AP that al-Libi's wife watched the raid unfold from her window.[6] At the time of this very public raid, Special Forces were only hours from also nabbing Benghazi ringleader Khattala, whom they'd been tracking for months, U.S. officials told CNN.[7]

It's bad enough al-Libi's capture was almost immediately leaked to the news media. Four days later, on October 9, the Obama administration strangely told the news media that the Libyan government had approved the al-Libi raid and also granted permission to seize Khattala. The details were splashed on the front page of the *New York Times* in a story titled "U.S. Officials Say Libya Approved Commando Raids." The article quotes "more than half a dozen American diplomatic, military, law enforcement, intelligence and other administration officials." Regarding the Libyan government's approval, the *Times* reports, "The Libyans' consent marks a significant step forward for the Obama administration, which has been criticized by Congressional Republicans for moving too slowly to apprehend the Benghazi suspects."[8]

In its reporting, the *Times* notes what is patently obvious: the leak of the al-Libi raid may have given Khattala a heads-up that his own capture was impending. Reported the *Times*, "While American officials expected that the Libyan government would claim that it had known nothing about the operation, news of the raid has raised concerns that the suspect in the Benghazi attacks, Ahmed Abu Khattala, has now been tipped off that the United States has the ability to conduct an operation in Libya." Even the *Times* was puzzled, writing, "It is not clear why American military commanders did not conduct both operations simultaneously to avoid this problem."[9]

Indeed, U.S. Forces may have been ready to act to capture Khattala as soon as the day after al-Libi's arrest, according to some officials speaking to CNN. The news network revealed a top-level White House meeting was scheduled for around October 7 to get Obama's final approval to capture Khattala.[10] However, al-Libi's capture and its subsequent leak to news media sent Khattala underground and further caused a major rift with the Libyan government, which demanded an end to any future U.S. raids.

CNN reported the Khattala raid never materialized

"partly because there was so much publicity inside Libya and in the Western press about the al-Libi capture."[11] The publicity about al-Libi's capture was nearly unavoidable since U.S. forces for some reason seized the wanted terrorist in broad daylight instead of capturing him in a more secretive manner.

CNN related that the aborted Khattala capture is leading "to sensitive questions inside the administration about the tradeoff between getting al-Libi and going after the perpetrators of the politically charged Benghazi attack." Obama had previously vowed to make it a "priority" to bring the Benghazi suspects "to justice."

In its October 9 front-page piece, the *New York Times* disclosed that the efforts to track Khattala had been in place for months. The newspaper further reported the Pentagon "has been preparing contingency plans for months in the event Mr. Obama orders a military operation" to seize Khattala and other terrorists for the Benghazi attack.[12]

Unfortunately for Libyan prime minister Ali Zeidan, the publicity surrounding al-Libi's capture created such a backlash for him that he was reportedly briefly kidnapped in retaliation for allowing the United States to act on Libyan soil.

Washington Post opinion writer Mark Thiessen took issue with the Obama administration's leak to the *New York Times* about the Libyan government's approval of al-Libi's capture. "With the leak that the Libyans approved both raids, and the kidnapping of the Libyan prime minister, [Khattala's] government probably will not authorize more such operations for the foreseeable future," he wrote.[13]

Indeed, in December 2013, the *Washington Post* featured an update on Khattala, making it crystal clear the decision to capture al-Libi may leave Khattala free to live in jihadist paradise in Libya for quite some time to come. It is increasingly unlikely the United States will have another opportunity to capture him anytime soon, the paper said. One official told the *Post* that Khattala is operating in eastern Libya with impunity. "He's as free as a bird," the official complained.[14]

The *Post* recalled the mission to capture Khattala was scrapped after al-Libi's seizure, and any plans to remove him from Libya were put on the back burner. American officials claimed that another raid to seize Khattala could "lead to the toppling of Zeidan's government and increase the chaos in a country that the United States would like to see stabilize."

But Rep. Mike Rogers (R-MI), who chairs the House Intelligence Committee, isn't buying it. "I don't subscribe to that theory, and that is a theory," Rogers told the *Post*.[15]

It makes little sense that the Obama administration decided to expose details of the Libyan government's approval of the raids. The leak was sure to inflame Zeidan. The method of capturing al-Libi in broad daylight while his family watched seemed almost designed to attract attention from both the news media and the terrorist community in Libya. It doesn't take a tactical genius to understand that as soon as al-Libi's very public capture was inevitably made known, jihadists throughout Libya would go dark. And once it was announced that Zeidan's administration had rubber-stamped the raids, the resulting pressure against him to not allow future capture operations was almost sure to come.

Too much just doesn't add up.

7

GAME CHANGER: HILLARY'S CENTRAL, UNREPORTED ROLE IN BENGHAZI

Observers of the Benghazi scandal are quite familiar with the generalities of Hillary Clinton's infamous testimony before the Senate Foreign Relations Committee. Clinton's reaction to the murderous September 11, 2012, Benghazi attacks will forever be remembered by eight insulting words: "What difference at this point does it make?!"[1] This infuriated response was fired at a lawmaker who dared to press her on why four Americans, including a sitting U.S. ambassador, were murdered. Clinton's testimony that day, and specifically her shocking "what difference" jibe, has become so associated with the attacks that the image of her testimony is one of the most frequently returned pictures in Google whenever a user types in the word "Benghazi."

However, despite Clinton's very public display of what many see as arrogance in the face of a legitimate line of inquisition, few are aware of the central role she played in the real Benghazi scandal, from her direct involvement in approving lawful occupancy of the disgracefully unsecured U.S. special mission, to the weapons-to-rebels scheme, to the very reason Ambassador Chris Stevens was in the compound on the dangerous day of 9/11 in the first place. We are herein going to document Clinton's undeniably fundamental role in virtually the entire Benghazi story, replete with information indicating she may have perjured herself during sworn testimony.

PULLED CRITICAL SECURITY

Let's start with Clinton's personal approval of security conditions at the compound. By this point you are familiar with the stunning backwardness of the U.S. special mission's so-called security posture. Guard towers were denied; a special reaction team was pulled from Libya's hot zone; an aircraft was recalled. External protection of the compound was provided entirely by poorly trained, unarmed local Libyans who had virtually no capabilities to fend off armed attackers. Internal security was incomprehensibly left to the devices of armed members of the February 17 Martyrs Brigade militia, a ragtag group affiliated with the al-Qaeda–linked, Islamic extremist Ansar al-Sharia terrorist organization that was later implicated in the Benghazi assault. Despite numerous previous strikes against both the U.S. special mission and other Western compounds in Benghazi, and in spite of a large number of requests from U.S. diplomats on the ground, there was little change in the dismal state of "security" at the mission.

Yet it can now be said that Clinton personally provided the legal waivers for U.S. personnel to occupy that death trap of a mission. This largely unreported detail was confirmed in the Senate's January 2014 report on Benghazi. Senate investigators found the Benghazi facility required a special waiver since it did not meet the minimum official security standards set by the State Department.

Some of the necessary waivers, the Senate affirmed, could have been issued at lower levels within the State Department. However "other departures, such as the co-location requirement, could only be approved by the Secretary of State."[2] The "co-location" requirement refers to an unusual housing setup in Benghazi where intelligence and State Department personnel were kept in two separate locations. Traditionally, intelligence personnel operate from official State buildings, such as embassies and consulates. This means Clinton herself approved some aspects of the U.S. special mission, including separating the mission from the seemingly more protected CIA annex. In doing so, did Clinton know she was approving a woefully unprotected compound? If not, then at the very least she is guilty of dereliction of duty and the diplomatic equivalent of criminal negligence.

It has emerged that top deputies working directly under Clinton, including officials known to be close to the ambitious politicians, were single-handedly responsible for some of the most shocking security decisions made regarding the Benghazi compound. It is difficult to imagine, indeed it is entirely nonsensical to argue that these Clinton deputies were acting without her direct knowledge and permission, especially in the central theater of Libya, the linchpin of the so-called Arab Spring.

In chapter 1, we documented that four months before the attack, State Department under secretary Patrick Kennedy canceled the use in Tripoli of a DC-3 aircraft that could have aided in the evacuation of the Benghazi victims. Kennedy also nonsensically denied guard towers to the Benghazi mission and approved the withdrawal of a Security Support Team (or SST, special U.S. forces specifically maintained for counterattacks on U.S. embassies or threats against diplomatic personnel).[3] Remember the decision to withdraw the SST was made "despite compelling requests from personnel in Libya that the team be allowed to stay."[4] These details and more were contained in a scathing February 2014 report by Republicans on the House Foreign Affairs Committee.

That same House Republican report further noted it was Kennedy who in December 2011 approved a one-year extension of the Benghazi mission despite major security lapses at the building. The State Department's ARB report, while not mentioning Kennedy by name, itself conceded there was a "flawed process by which Special Mission Benghazi's extension until the end of December 2012 was approved," admitting it was "a decision that did not take security considerations adequately into account."[5]

A January Senate report further assailed Kennedy for declining an offer from the Department of Defense (DoD) to "sustain or provide additional DoD security personnel in

Libya by extending the deployment of the DoD Site Security Team in Tripoli, transitioning to a Marine Security Detachment, or deploying a U.S. Marine Corps Fleet Antiterrorism Security Team."[6]

Now, which security-conscious individual would decline an offer from the military to protect the Benghazi compound? The Senate report cited information that not only was Kennedy fully aware of the lack of security in Benghazi, he also "approved every person who went to Libya and received a daily report on the number of personnel, their names, and their status."[7]

Even the ARB, known for minimizing Clinton's complacency in the attacks, states unnamed State officials are guilty of "systemic failures and leadership and management deficiencies" that contributed to the "grossly inadequate" security situation in Benghazi.[8] Unbashful House Republicans had no problem naming those State officials, all of whom served directly under Clinton. The four officials were revealed to be Assistant Secretary for Diplomatic Security Eric Boswell, Principal Deputy Assistant Secretary of Diplomatic Security Scott Bultrowicz, Deputy Assistant Secretary of Diplomatic Security for International Programs Charlene Lamb, and Deputy Assistant Secretary for Maghreb Affairs Raymond Maxwell.[9]

Despite the State Department's proclamations that those responsible would be disciplined or removed, as of this writing three of the officials were reassigned to new posts.[10] Maxwell voluntarily retired, something he had planned to do in 2012 but had postponed due to regional turmoil during the Arab Spring.[11] Maxwell was later found to not have contributed to security decisions in Benghazi, while the other three officials were reportedly involved in those ultimately disastrous decisions.[12]

The Senate singled out Charlene Lamb, who worked closely with Clinton, for her "unwillingness to provide additional security personnel" to the Benghazi facility.[13]

Not only were Clinton's deputies the ones who made the security decisions, they were also involved in later drafting the now discredited talking points on the Benghazi attacks. State Department spokesperson Victoria Nuland "played an active role" in crafting those talking points and got promoted to assistant secretary for European and Eurasian Affairs. Clinton's deputy chief of staff, Jake Sullivan, was also a point man in shaping the talking points.[14] Interestingly ex-CIA official Mike Morell, a central player in the talking points scandal, took a job as a counselor to Beacon Global Strategies, a consulting group known for its close ties to Clinton.[15]

After reviewing the direct involvement of these Clinton deputies, which of these possibilities do you consider the most likely: Clinton was head-deep in the fatal security posture of the Benghazi mission, or she was unaware of the lack of security that was her own department's doing? If the latter is the real situation, then someone had better summon the ghost of Sen. Joe McCarthy because it would mean rogue elements hijacked the State Department to deny security to the Benghazi mission without the knowledge of the secretary of state.

If Clinton, however, was apprised of the security situation in the Benghazi facility, which was largely handled by her own deputies, then she may have misled lawmakers and the public under oath when she testified on January 23, 2013, that no one within the government ever recommended the closure of the U.S. facilities in the Libyan city. In her testimony, Clinton stated: "Well, Senator, I want to make clear that no one in the State Department, the intelligence community, any other agency ever recommended that we close Benghazi. We were clear-eyed . . . about the . . . threats and the dangers as they were developing in Eastern Libya, and in Benghazi."[16] Clinton was responding to a question from Sen. Jeff Flake (R-AZ).

Clinton's testimony is contradicted by Lt. Col. Andrew Wood, who led the U.S. military's efforts to supplement diplomatic security in Libya. Wood testified that he personally recommended the Benghazi mission be closed, as documented in the forty-six-page House Republican report probing the Benghazi attacks. Page 6 of the report cites security concerns, including more than two hundred attacks in Libya, fifty of which took place in Benghazi, including against the U.S. mission there.

States the Republican report: "These developments caused Lieutenant Colonel Andrew Wood, who led the U.S. military's efforts to supplement diplomatic security in Libya, to recommend that the State Department consider pulling out of Benghazi altogether. Lieutenant Colonel Wood explained that after the withdrawal of these other organizations, 'it was apparent to me that we were the last [Western] flag flying in Benghazi. We were the last thing on their target list to remove from Benghazi.'"[17]

In particularly stinging comments, an updated House report concluded that "at the end of the day, [Clinton] was responsible for ensuring the safety of all Americans serving in our diplomatic facilities. Her failure to do so clearly made a difference in the lives of the four murdered Americans and their families."[18]

CLINTON SENT STEVENS INTO DOOMED MISSION?

Besides responsibility for the unfathomable withdrawal and subsequent denial of security at the U.S. special mission, Clinton may have played a role in Stevens' decision to go to the dangerous facility on the anniversary of the 9/11 terrorist attacks, a day when jihadists are particularly motivated to strike our country's assets. This largely unreported role prompts larger questions about Clinton's national security decisions and her possible disregard of clear, present, and obvious terrorist threats.

In several previous chapters we documented that al-Qaeda and other Islamic extremist groups gained major ground in Libya following U.S. intervention there to the point that they were establishing training camps in Benghazi. Things took such a turn that those al-Qaeda–linked groups, including the parent organization of the February 17 Martyrs Brigade, held a Sharia Islamic law confab not far from the Benghazi mission. Clinton and the U.S. diplomatic staff in Libya were aware of the terrorist camps in Benghazi. Fox News reported the U.S. mission in Benghazi convened an "emergency meeting" in August 2012 to discuss the training camps. The news network obtained a government cable addressed to Clinton's office stating that the U.S. diplomats in Libya were briefed "on the location of approximately ten Islamist militias and AQ training camps within Benghazi . . . These groups ran the spectrum from Islamist militias, such as the QRF Brigade and Ansar al-Sharia, to 'Takfirist thugs.'"[19] This borders on the surreal. After being briefed about nearby terrorist training facilities, no action was taken to secure the U.S. compound.

Remember that Libya was supposed to be the prototype of the so-called Arab Spring, a shining beacon of democracy for other Arab and Middle Eastern countries to emulate. Instead, the country descended into chaos, with extremist groups moving quickly to fill the void. Despite this deteriorating and well-reported security situation, Clinton actually worked on plans to declare a symbolic victory in Benghazi. According to congressional testimony by Gregory Hicks, the former State Department deputy chief of mission and chargé d'affairs, who was in Libya at the time of the attack, Stevens went to the compound that day in part because Clinton wanted to convert the shanty complex "into a permanent constituent post" as a symbol of the new Libya. "Timing for this decision was important," Hicks explained. "Chris needed to report before September 30th, the end of the fiscal year, on the physical—the political and security environment in

Benghazi to support an action memo to convert Benghazi from a temporary facility to a permanent facility."[20]

Hicks revealed the directive to convert the compound came from the State Department Office of Near Eastern Affairs, headed by acting assistant secretary Beth Jones. Money was available to be transferred to Benghazi from a State Department fund set aside for Iraq, provided the funds transfer was done by September 30.

He further testified that in May 2012, during a meeting with Clinton, Stevens promised he would give priority to making sure the U.S. facility at Benghazi was transformed into a permanent constituent post. Hicks said Stevens himself "wanted to make a symbolic gesture to the people of Benghazi that the United States stood behind their dream of establishing a new democracy."[21]

Toward the end of the hearing, the chairman, Rep. Darrell Issa (R-CA), asked Hicks to summarize his testimony on why Stevens went to Benghazi. "At least one of the reasons he was in Benghazi was to further the secretary's wish that, that post become a permanent constituent post, and also there, because we understood the secretary intended to visit Tripoli later in the year," Hicks reiterated. "We hoped that she would be able to announce to the Libyan people our establishment of a permanent constituent post in Benghazi at that time."[22]

ARMS-TO-JIHADISTS

We can only venture to guess the motivation for Clinton's deputies to repeatedly reject necessary protection to the U.S.

special mission while withdrawing aircraft and even a special response team from one of the most endangered State Department posts in the world. Some conspiracy theorists have baselessly claimed the government wanted Stevens dead and set out to deliberately sabotage the mission. Aside from there being no evidence to support this wild charge, the accusation simply doesn't make sense on several levels. Why would the State Department want to kill Stevens? He wasn't threatening to divulge the secretive activities taking place inside the facility. In fact, he was one of the central figures in the arms-to-rebels scheme. To briefly entertain this horrible conspiracy for the purposes of refuting it, let's say someone did want Stevens killed. There are far cleaner ways to achieve that sickening goal. It's pretty time-consuming and even highly conspicuous to deny security to the mission for months while setting up the mission to invite such an attack just to have our ambassador terminated. Plus, we'd have to believe the attackers were directed on some level by the U.S. government, a pretty outrageous assumption.

The State Department would further have to be run by unskilled idiots to use the assault to kill Stevens. The attack was an utter embarrassment to the State Department, caused a major political scandal, and only served to draw more attention to what was transpiring inside the secretive facility, a compound the United States went to great lengths to hide. Instead, for those who do want to entertain this conspiracy, it would have been far easier and cleaner to have Stevens taken out in a roadside bombing or sniper attack, both of which are regular occurrences in Benghazi. That said, let's get back to reality. I believe a more likely explanation for the denial of security was to keep the U.S. mission's activities secretive, perhaps even obscured from the military, which repeatedly offered to beef up protection at the compound.

Clinton, it seems, was not only personally involved in some of those alleged activities, primarily the arms-to-jihadists scheme; she was a ringleader. In fact, in February 2013, the *New York Times* described Clinton as one of the driving forces behind advocating a plan to arm the Syrian rebels. Specifically, Clinton's plan—which was also proposed by then CIA director David Petraeus and then defense secretary Leon E. Panetta—called for rebel groups to be vetted, trained, and armed "with the assistance of some neighboring states."[23]

The newspaper quoted White House officials claiming they rejected the plan; however, it is difficult to believe the White House would reject a plan proposed and supported by the secretaries of state and defense—plus the CIA chief, to boot. Furthermore, another *Times* report one month later confirmed American-aided arms were shipped to the rebels for weeks. The paper's description of the arms shipments mirrors the exact plan as reportedly concocted by Clinton.

The *Times* reported that since at least November 2012, the United States had been helping "the Arab governments shop for weapons, including a large procurement from Croatia, and have vetted rebel commanders and groups to determine who should receive the weapons as they arrive."[24]

In other words, Clinton's plan to arm the rebels was seemingly put into action.

If this is the case—and all the evidence points there (see chapter 2 for more)—then Clinton has even more explaining to do because she claimed during her Benghazi testimony that she did not know whether the U.S. mission in Libya was procuring or transferring weapons to Turkey and other Arab countries.

Sen. Rand Paul (R-KY) asked Clinton a pretty direct question: "Is the U.S. involved with any procuring of weapons, transfer of weapons, buying, selling, anyhow transferring weapons to Turkey out of Libya?"

"To Turkey?" Clinton asked, as her voice suddenly jumped an octave. "I will have to take that question for the record. Nobody has ever raised that with me."

Continued Paul: "It's been in news reports that ships have been leaving from Libya and that may have weapons, and what I'd like to know is the annex that was close by, were they involved with procuring, buying, selling, obtaining weapons, and were any of these weapons being transferred to other countries, any countries, Turkey included?"

Clinton replied, "Well, senator, you'll have to direct that question to the agency that ran the annex. I will see what information is available."

"You're saying you don't know?" asked Paul.

"I do not know," Clinton said. "I don't have any information on that."[25]

So we are to believe that Clinton did not know her

plan to arm the rebels was put into action as her State Department underlings pulled critical security from the Benghazi mission while denying repeated requests for the bare-minimum protection at the strangely established compound located in al-Qaedaville, where she was set to declare victory in Libya as jihadists set up training camps and looted missiles. I'll buy that bridge now.

8

THE *REAL* STORY OF THOSE PESKY TALKING POINTS

An enormous amount of attention has been centered on the Obama administration's altering of the now-infamous talking points on Benghazi, scrubbing references to terrorism while stressing a so-called popular protest against an obscure, anti-Islam film. The protest, by most accounts, never took place and certainly had nothing to do with the motivation for the assault.

The talking points scandal goes beyond the selective editing of intelligence information or the cover-ups of the well-coordinated jihadist assault. The implications of the duplicitous editing affair are larger than obscuring the possibly illicit activities taking place inside the U.S. special mission. The story here is the large-scale, purposeful deception of the American public, the abject betrayal of public trust to the point that national security was willingly jeopardized by stirring further riots across the Islamic world when the government decided to draw more attention to the Muhammad film and even to use taxpayer dollars to apologize for the irrelevant movie. After top administration officials were caught crafting misleading talking points, they boxed themselves in even further by lying about why the points were selectively edited, claiming the changes were made to prevent compromising an ongoing criminal investigation.

The curious talking points tale began when U.S. intelligence officials testified behind closed doors in early November 2012 and were asked point-blank whether they had altered the material on which United Nations ambassador Susan Rice had based her original statements to the public about the Benghazi attacks. On Sunday, September 16, 2012, Rice had appeared on five morning television programs to offer the official Obama administration response to the Benghazi attacks. In nearly identical statements, she asserted that the attacks were a spontaneous protest in response to a "hateful video."[1] Other Obama administration officials made similar claims.

Four days after Rice's misinformation, at a town-hall event hosted by Univision, Obama himself was questioned about whether the Benghazi attack was carried out by terrorists. He responded, "What we do know is that the natural protests that arose because of the outrage over the video were used as an excuse by extremists to see if they can also directly harm U.S. interests." Pressed about whether al-Qaeda was behind the assault, he replied, "Well, we don't know yet."[2]

It would later emerge that the talking points were

edited to remove references to terrorism and al-Qaeda in the attacks. The administration also removed information about at least five other attacks against foreign interests in Benghazi.[3] An original draft stating, "We do know that Islamic extremists with ties to al-Qa'ida participated in the attack" was changed to "We do know that Islamic extremists participated in the violent demonstrations."[4] Note the replacement of "attack" with "violent demonstrations."

Of course, the United States immediately had surveillance video from the mission that showed there was no popular protest at all on September 11, 2012. Gregory Hicks, the No. 2 U.S. official in Libya at the time of the September 11, 2012, attacks, testified that he knew immediately the attacks were terror strikes, not a protest turned violent. According to Hicks, "everybody in the mission" believed it was an act of terror "from the get-go."[5]

The day after the attack, Libya's deputy ambassador to London, Ahmad Jibril, told the BBC that Ansar al-Sharia carried out the assault.[6] Libyan president Mohammed el-Megarif was even more direct, saying foreigner jihadists who infiltrated Libya planned the attack and used some local Libyans during the event. "The idea that this criminal and cowardly act was a spontaneous protest that just spun out of control is completely unfounded and preposterous," he said. "We firmly believe that this was a precalculated, preplanned attack that was carried out specifically to attack the U.S. Consulate."[7]

Obviously logic dictates that spontaneous protesters

do not show up with weapons, erect armed checkpoints surrounding a compound, and show insider knowledge of the facility while deploying military-style tactics to storm a U.S. mission. Nor do they know the exact location of a secretive CIA annex, including the specific coordinates of the building that were likely utilized to launch precision mortar strikes. Spontaneous protesters are not capable of mounting a fierce, hours-long gun battle with U.S. forces stationed inside the annex. And yet, the Obama administration was willing to reject logic and its own knowledge of what really happened to lie outright to the American people.

Two congressional sources who spoke to Reuters on condition of anonymity said that Mike Morell, then acting CIA director, along with director of national intelligence James Clapper, and National Counterterrorism Center director Matthew Olsen, each testified behind closed doors that they did not alter the talking points. On November 16, 2012, former CIA director David Petraeus testified before the same congressional intelligence committees and also replied no to the question of whether he had changed the talking points, three congressional sources told Reuters.[8]

Then things got interesting on November 27 when, according to senators who met with Morell that day, the CIA reportedly told lawmakers it had in fact changed the wording of the unclassified talking points to delete a reference to al-Qaeda. That November 27 meeting was between Morell, Rice, and Republican senators John McCain, Lindsey Graham, and Kelly Ayotte. A statement by McCain,

Graham, and Ayotte specifically related that Morell told them during the meeting that the FBI had removed references to al-Qaeda from the talking points "and did so to prevent compromising an ongoing criminal investigation" of the attack on the U.S. mission. The senators said in the joint statement, "We were surprised by this revelation and the reasoning behind it."[9]

Morell's claim of changing the talking points to protect a criminal investigation was repeated to the news media. On November 28, 2012, intrepid CBS News reporter Sharyl Attkisson, who resigned from the news agency in March 2014, quoted the CIA stating the edits to the talking points were made "so as not to tip off al Qaeda as to what the U.S. knew, and to protect sources and methods." That same report quoted a source from the Office of the Director for National Intelligence, aka James Clapper, telling CBS News' Margaret Brennan that Clapper's office made the edits as part of the interagency process because the links to al-Qaeda were deemed too "tenuous" to make public.[10]

Meanwhile, a few hours after his meeting with the senators, Morell's office reportedly contacted Graham to backtrack, claiming that "Acting Director Morell misspoke" in the earlier meeting. "The CIA now says that it deleted the al-Qaeda references, not the FBI. They were unable to give a reason as to why," Graham said in a statement.[11]

An intelligence official called Morell's change "an honest mistake and it was corrected as soon as it was realized. There is nothing more to this."[12] And CBS News was told that there was "absolutely no intent to misinform." The official speaking to CBS claimed the talking points "were never meant to be definitive and, in fact, noted that the assessment may change. The points clearly reflect the early indications of extremist involvement in a direct result. It wasn't until after they were used in public that analysts reconciled contradictory information about how the assault began."[13]

Graham at the time went so far as to suggest he would hold up the nomination of Morell if Obama pushed him for CIA director, a position ultimately filled by John Brennon. All of the sudden, in June 2013, Morell announced he was stepping down to spend more time with his family. In a statement, Morell acknowledged that his reason for stepping down may seem somewhat difficult to swallow, but "when I say that it is time for my family, nothing could be more real than that."[14] Morell had served thirty-three years in the agency and was a front-runner for CIA director; it is doubtful he resigned to become a family man. As noted in the previous chapter, he later reemerged as a counselor to Beacon Global Strategies, an advisory firm particularly close to Hillary Clinton.[15] The firm is led by Philippe I. Reines, who served from 2009 to 2013 as Clinton's deputy assistant secretary of state for strategic communications and senior communications advisor.[16]

In February 2014 a bipartisan Senate Intelligence Committee report revealed that Morell was in receipt of critical information on September 15, 2012, one day before Rice used the talking points publicly. The report said that Morell and others at the CIA received an e-mail from the CIA's Libya station chief stating the attacks were "not an escalation of protests." So on the same day Morell had helped edit the talking points by calling the attacks a "demonstration," he had received correspondence from his own station chief clearly contradicting this claim. Sam Faddis, an expert on the U.S. intelligence community, explained to Fox News, "The chief of station is the senior intelligence officer for the entire United States government. You would really have to have some incredibly overwhelming factual evidence to disregard that and there is no indication of that in the report at all."[17]

GOP CHARGES OBAMA OFFICIALS LIED TO PROTECT STATE

In perhaps one of the most damning sections of the Republican House Interim Progress Report on the events in Benghazi, lawmakers who penned the investigation wrote that they were given access to classified e-mails and other communications that prove the talking points were edited to protect none other than the State Department's own reputation. "Evidence rebuts Administration claims that the talking points were modified to protect classified information or to protect an investigation by the Federal Bureau of Investigation (FBI)," the report states, directly contradicting Morell's claims.[18]

It is instructive to briefly quote the report:

> *To protect the State Department*, the Administration *deliberately* removed references to al-Qa'ida-linked groups and previous attacks in Benghazi in the talking points used by [United Nations] Ambassador [Susan] Rice,

> thereby perpetuating the deliberately misleading and incomplete narrative that the attacks evolved from a demonstration caused by a YouTube video. . . .
>
> Senior State Department officials requested—and the White House approved—that the details of the threats, specifics of the previous attacks, and previous warnings be removed to insulate the department from criticism that it ignored the threat environment in Benghazi.[19]

The interim House report authors said that as they went through e-mail exchanges of the interagency process to scrub the talking points, the e-mails did not reveal any concern with protecting classified information. "Additionally, the Bureau [FBI] itself approved a version of the talking points with significantly more information about the attacks and previous threats than the version that the State Department requested. Thus, the claim that the State Department's edits were made solely to protect that investigation is not credible."[20]

In a particularly stinging accusation, the report states: "When draft talking points were sent to officials throughout the Executive Branch, senior State Department officials requested the talking points be changed *to avoid criticism for ignoring the threat environment in Benghazi.* Specifically, State Department e-mails reveal senior officials had 'serious concerns' about the talking points, because Members of Congress might attack the State Department for 'not paying attention to agency warnings' about the growing threat in Benghazi."[21]

Of course, the House report barely scratches the surface of the possible motivations in hiding the true nature of the

Benghazi attacks from the American public. Besides ignoring the growing jihadist threats in Benghazi, the truth about the assault would have led to uncomfortable questions about why State not only denied security requests made by U.S. personnel on the ground but also strangely pulled critical protection while turning down Pentagon offers to provide more manpower at the facility. It may also have also prompted questions about why the al-Qaeda–linked February 17 Martyrs Brigade served as the mission's armed quick reaction force instead of specially trained U.S. forces. Recall the Benghazi attacks took place a few weeks before the 2012 presidential election. If any of this had been exposed before the election, Obama might not be the current White House occupant.

OBAMA, HILLARY USED TAXPAYER FUNDS IN BENGHAZI COVER-UP

Lying to the American public is bad enough. Adding insult to injury, the Obama administration's decision to blame the anti-Muhammad film for protests that never took place served to further inflame the Islamic world against the United States, escalating deadly rioting. The administration spent seventy thousand dollars in taxpayer funds on an ad campaign denouncing the film. The ads reportedly aired on seven Pakistani networks. The commercials also came in response to protests in Pakistan that were reportedly a reaction to the film. However, it was the claim of popular protests in Benghazi at the time that garnered the biggest public reaction from the White House.

The September 19, 2012, ads feature Obama and Clinton making statements against the film in the wake of the Benghazi attacks. "Since our founding, the United States has been a nation of respect, that respects all faiths. We reject all efforts to denigrate the religious beliefs of others," Obama says in the ad, which was stamped "Paid Content." Clinton then denies any official U.S. involvement in producing the "Innocence of Muslims" video. "We absolutely reject its contents," she says.[22]

In a clear bid to push the Muhammad film lie, law enforcement agents took the unusual and very public move of storming the home of Nakoula Basseley Nakoula, the man said to be behind the film, because he was accused of violating his probation from a 2010 check fraud conviction. The director was escorted from his house by authorities, in full view of news media cameras. A judge ordered Nakoula be held without bail.[23]

DID STATE DEPT. HIDE THIS DRAMATIC EVACUATION?

One astonishing, nearly unprecedented event that transpired in Benghazi the night of the attacks has been largely kept from the public. I am referring to a dramatic incident during the assault in which U.S. embassy staff four hundred miles away in Tripoli evacuated their residential compound under possible terror threat. The threat was taken so seriously that, according to a key embassy staffer, communications equipment was dismantled and hard drives were smashed with an axe.

The scene was first brought to light in congressional testimony by Gregory Hicks, the former U.S. deputy chief of mission in Libya. The incident was not mentioned in the State Department probe, nor was it previously reported in news accounts of the attack, including accounts of Hicks' testimony.[24]

Hicks said that about three hours after the attack began on the U.S. facility in Benghazi, the embassy staff in Tripoli noticed Twitter feeds asserting that the terror group Ansar al-Sharia was responsible. Hicks said there was also a call on the social media platform for an attack on the embassy in Tripoli." We had always thought that we were . . . under threat, that we now have to take care of ourselves, and we began planning to evacuate our facility," he said. "When I say our facility, I mean the State Department residential compound in Tripoli, and to consolidate all of our personnel . . . at the annex in Tripoli."

Hicks testified that he "immediately telephoned Washington that news afterwards and began accelerating our effort to withdraw from the Villas compound and move to the annex." He further recalled how his team had "responded with amazing discipline and courage in Tripoli in organizing withdrawal." Continued Hicks: "I have vivid memories of that. I think the most telling, though, was of our communications staff dismantling our communications equipment to take with us to the annex and destroying the classified communications capability.

"Our office manager, Amber Pickens, was everywhere that night just throwing herself into some task that had to be done," he went on. "First she was taking a log of what we were doing. Then she was loading magazines, carrying ammunition to the—carrying our ammunition supply to . . . our vehicles, and then she was smashing hard drives with an axe."

The vivid, nearly unprecedented scene, however, was not reported in the State Department's description of the Tripoli embassy's response the night of the Benghazi attack. The section of the State Department's ARB probe titled "Embassy Tripoli Response" simply says that upon notification of the attack in Benghazi, the U.S. embassy set up a command center and notified Washington.[25]

A later section in the State Department's probe describes how a seven-person response team from Tripoli arrived in Benghazi to lend support but could not get to the Benghazi facility due to a lack of transportation. The section also says the Tripoli embassy worked with the Libyan government to have a Libyan Air Force C-130 take the remaining U.S. government personnel from Benghazi to Tripoli.[26]

If the Obama administration could hide the dramatic evacuation of the Tripoli embassy while crafting misleading talking points to deceive the American public about the nature of the September 11, 2012 attacks, what else don't we know about the real Benghazi story?

9

NEWS MEDIA SNAGGED IN BENGHAZI DECEPTION

The news media's distortion of what happened in Benghazi on September 11, 2012, is so grandiose and the cover-up of Obama administration misdeeds so egregious that I could easily dedicate an entire book to exclusively correcting the misinformation and faulty reporting related to the coordinated terrorist assault. Since it is virtually impossible to squeeze all of these media misrepresentations into one chapter, I will instead focus on a few of the more outlandish examples of media malpractice. For the purposes of this chapter, I won't even attempt to document the mainstream news media reports that continue to wrongly call the attacked U.S. facility a "consulate" when it was anything but. Instead, let's take a look at the way major news agencies have been misleading the public on the narrative of what really happened.

NEW YORK TIMES CONTRADICTED BY . . . *NEW YORK TIMES*

Let's start with one of the most disgraceful pieces of propaganda in international "reporting" I have seen in quite some time. On December 28, 2013, *New York Times* reporter David D. Kirkpatrick released a book-length, multi-chapter article that sought to literally rewrite the entire Benghazi tale. The report, titled "A Deadly Mix in Benghazi," is filled with misleading information, including details negated by the U.S. government, Benghazi victims, and numerous previous news reports. In fact, I will show that Kirkpatrick's fanciful piece is scandalously contradicted by his *own* previous reportage.

One of the major contentions in Kirkpatrick's *Times* piece is that "contrary to claims by some members of Congress," the Benghazi attack "was fueled in large part by anger at an American-made video denigrating Islam."[1] He repeated in chapter 5 of the article, "There is no doubt that anger over the video motivated many attackers."[2] Another central claim is that there is "no evidence that Al Qaeda or other international terrorist groups had any role in the assault."[3] Laughably, Kirkpatrick seeks to prove the Benghazi attack was largely not premeditated, although the article allows that some aspects of the assault were loosely planned the day of the actual attack. I will now dismantle each of these claims, in part using the *Times'* own reporting.

Before we address the outlandish tale about the anti-Muhammad film, let's start with the contention that al-Qaeda or international jihadi organizations played no role in the assault, a claim that clearly seeks to bolster the Obama administration's thoroughly discredited talking points that infamously scrubbed terrorism as a motivating factor in the attacks. Stunningly, in his piece, Kirkpatrick asserts "Benghazi was not infiltrated by Al Qaeda, but nonetheless contained grave local threats to American interests."[4]

Benghazi was not infiltrated by al-Qaeda? The U.S. government may take issue with that. Recall chapter 5, where we documented how a Library of Congress report detailed—one month before the deadly September 11 attack in Benghazi—that al-Qaeda established a major base of operations in Libya in the aftermath of the U.S.-NATO campaign that deposed Muammar Gaddafi and his secular regime. The report warned that al-Qaeda and affiliated organizations were establishing terrorist training camps and pushing Taliban-style Islamic law in Libya while the new, Western-backed Libyan government incorporated jihadists into its militias. The document said scores of Islamic extremists were freed from Libyan prison after the U.S.-supported revolution in Libya.[5]

Embarrassingly for Kirkpatrick, the claim of no al-Qaeda infiltration in Benghazi is contradicted by another *Times* article, to which he contributed reporting from Benghazi. That's right. An October 29, 2012, *New York Times* article titled "Libya Warnings Were Plentiful, but Unspecific" related that "Al Qaeda-leaning" Islamic extremists were establishing training camps in the mountains near Benghazi.[6]

The 2012 article begins: "In the months leading up to

the Sept. 11 attacks on the American diplomatic mission in Benghazi, the Obama administration received intelligence reports that Islamic extremist groups were operating training camps in the mountains near the Libyan city and that some of the fighters were 'Al Qaeda-leaning,' according to American and European officials."[7]

Continued the *Times* article:

> Small-scale camps grew out of training areas created last year by militias fighting Libyan government security forces. After the government fell, these compounds continued to churn out fighters trained in marksmanship and explosives, American officials said.
>
> Ansar al-Shariah, a local militant group some of whose members had ties to Al Qaeda in the Islamic Maghreb, a local Qaeda affiliate, operated a militant training camp whose location was well known to Benghazi residents. On the Friday after the attack, demonstrators overran it.
>
> American intelligence agencies had provided the administration with reports for much of the past year warning that the Libyan government was weakening and had little control over the militias, including Ansar al-Shariah.[8]

Things only get worse for Kirkpatrick. In his distorted "A Deadly Mix in Benghazi," the *Times* reporter claims the attacks were largely not premeditated, although again he does allow that some parts of the assault were loosely planned that day. "Surveillance of the American compound appears to have been underway at least 12 hours before the assault started," reported Kirkpatrick in his rewrite of history. "The violence, though, also had spontaneous elements. Anger at the video motivated the initial attack."

The journalist continued: "Looters and arsonists, without any sign of a plan, were the ones who ravaged the compound after the initial attack, according to more than a dozen Libyan witnesses as well as many American officials who have viewed the footage from security cameras."[9]

Both of Kirkpatrick's major contentions—that al-Qaeda was not involved and that the attack was largely not premeditated—are contradicted by a piece he cowrote with Steven Lee Myers on September 12, 2012, titled "Libya Attack Brings Challenges for U.S."[10] That's right. Kirkpatrick is so committed to his revisionist narrative he is willing to basically repudiate his own reporting without batting an eyebrow.

The article says: "Islamist militants armed with antiaircraft weapons and rocket-propelled grenades stormed a lightly defended United States diplomatic mission in Benghazi, Libya." The two writers added, "The assailants seemed organized, well trained and heavily armed, and they appeared to have at least some level of advance planning." Further contrasting with Kirkpatrick's later piece, the article went on to quote Col. Wolfgang Pusztai, Austria's former defense attaché to Libya, as saying he believed the attack "was 'deliberately planned and executed' by about a core group of 30 to 40 assailants who were 'well trained and organized.'"[11]

The "assault was led by a brigade of Islamist fighters known as Ansar al-Sharia, or the Supporters of Islamic Law," the writers informed. "Brigade members emphasized at the time that they were not acting alone." Ansar al-Sharia, as you well know by now, is an al-Qaeda–linked group.

Kirkpatrick and Myers continued: "On Wednesday, perhaps apprehensive over Mr. Stevens' death, the brigade said in a statement that its supporters 'were not officially involved or were not ordered to be involved' in the attack.

"At the same time, the brigade praised those who protested as 'the best of the best' of the Libyan people and supported their response to the video 'in the strongest possible terms.'"

More al-Qaeda and organized extremist connections to the Benghazi attack were reported by the *Daily Beast*, which confirmed an October 2012 *Wall Street Journal* report that fighters affiliated with the Egypt-based, al-Qaeda–linked Jamal Network group participated in the Benghazi attack.[12] Later on, the eighty-five-page Senate report on the Benghazi attacks, released January 2014, would confirm Jamal's involvement.[13]

Kirkpatrick's claim that the attacks were mostly not premeditated doesn't fit with the State ARB investigation into Benghazi, either. The ARB described a well-orchestrated attack with militants who seemingly had specific knowledge of the compound. The State investigation focused on "men armed with AK rifles" who "started to destroy the living room contents and then approached the safe area gate and started banging on it."[14]

In another detail bespeaking a plan, the ARB stated that the intruders smoked up Villa C, likely to make breathing so difficult that anyone inside the safe room where Ambassador Chris Stevens was holed up would need to come out.[15]

It may be further difficult for keen observers to swallow the *Times*' claim of unplanned looters in light of events that demonstrated the attackers knew the location of the nearby CIA annex or that they set up checkpoints, as they did, to ensure against the escape by Americans inside the special mission. In fact, as you may recall from chapter 4, they seemed to know where *everything* was, right down to the gasoline, the generators—and the precise location of Stevens' safe room.

Now let's get to Kirkpatrick's clownish claim that the Benghazi attacks were motivated by an anti-Muhammad film. First, the storyline simply doesn't jibe with an independent investigation that reportedly found no mention of the film on social media in Libya in the three days leading up to the attack. Agincourt Solutions, the leading social media monitoring firm, reviewed more than four thousand postings and found that the first reference to the film was not detected on social media until the day after the attack.[16]

The *Times*' claim of popular protests about the Muhammad film doesn't hold up to logic. The U.S. special mission was not a permanent facility, nor was its existence widely known by the public in Libya. Indeed, the State Department's ARB report on the Benghazi attack itself documented the facility was set up secretively and without the knowledge of the new Libyan government.

Kirkpatrick may not have realized it, but he undermined

his own claims about the Muhammad film later in the article, where he may have inadvertently alluded to some of the real motivation for the attackers. Interestingly, Kirkpatrick's article seeks to link the Benghazi attack to protests planned outside the U.S. embassy in Cairo. Reads the *Times* piece: "[O]n Sept. 8, a popular Islamist preacher lit the fuse by screening a clip of the video on the ultraconservative Egyptian satellite channel El Nas. American diplomats in Cairo raised the alarm in Washington about a growing backlash, including calls for a protest outside their embassy."[17]

However, as we extensively covered in chapter 5, the Cairo protest on September 11 was announced days in advance as part of a movement to free the so-called blind sheikh, Omar Abdel-Rahman, held in the United States over the 1993 World Trade Center bombing. The State Department's ARB report stated that the "Omar Abdurrahman group" was involved in previous attacks against diplomatic facilities in Benghazi.[18] Kirkpatrick failed to report that the anti-U.S. protest movement outside the Cairo embassy was a long-term project about freeing Rahman.

On the day of the September 11, 2012, protests in Cairo, CNN's Nic Robertson interviewed Rahman's son, who described the protest as being about freeing his father. No Muhammad film was mentioned. A big banner calling for Rahman's release can be seen as Robertson walked to the embassy protests.

ASSOCIATED PRESS BATTLES REUTERS

The case study of Kirkpatrick is simply the tip of the iceberg. There are legitimate questions about a Reuters article penned in the immediate aftermath of the jihadist attack against the U.S. mission in Benghazi.

Reads the September 12, 2012, Reuters report: "Accounts from Libyan and U.S. officials, and from locals who watched what began as a protest on Tuesday against a crudely made American film that insults the Prophet Mohammad spiral into violence and a military-style assault on U.S. troops, point to a series of unfortunate choices amid the confusion and fear." The article then quotes one protester—identified only as "a 17-year-old student named Hamam"—as saying, "When we had heard that there was a film that was insulting to the Prophet, we, as members of the public, and not as militia brigades, we came to the consulate here to protest and hold a small demonstration."[19]

"Hamam" further claimed that a rumor had spread that a protester had been wounded by firing from inside the U.S. mission, and so Hamam and many others "went off to retrieve guns" which, Reuters reported, "like many Libyans, they keep at home for security."

In other words, Reuters expects us to believe a bunch of local Libyan civilian protesters congregated outside the mission to protest an obscure film, and then, after a rumor had spread about an injured protester, these locals went home to retrieve weapons, only to return as expert warriors with inside knowledge of the compound. They then established armed and manned checkpoints around the U.S. mission, engaged in hours of fierce gun battles, overran the compound, knew about the existence of a secretive CIA annex, and even had mortars prepared to be fired at the second U.S. facility.

The news agency further reported: "Some of those who took part in the initial demonstration in Benghazi insisted it was a spontaneous, unplanned public protest which had begun relatively peacefully. Anger over the film also saw an unruly protest at the U.S. embassy across the Egyptian border in Cairo on Tuesday evening, with protesters scaling the walls." Of course, as noted both in this chapter and earlier in this book, the Cairo protests showed no signs of being about the film.

The version of events presented by Reuters would later be somewhat contradicted by an October 27, 2012, Associated Press report also based on a firsthand witness account. Reports the AP:

> It began around nightfall on Sept. 11 with around 150 bearded gunmen, some wearing the Afghan-style tunics favored by Islamic militants, sealing off the streets leading to the U.S. Consulate in Benghazi. They set up roadblocks with pick-up trucks mounted with heavy machine guns, according to witnesses.
>
> The trucks bore the logo of Ansar al-Shariah, a powerful local group of Islamist militants who worked with the municipal government to manage security in Benghazi, the main city in eastern Libya and birthplace of the uprising last year that ousted Moammar Gadhafi after a 42-year dictatorship.

Clearly contradicting the Reuters witness, the AP reported, "There was no sign of a spontaneous protest against an American-made movie denigrating Islam's Prophet Muhammad. But a lawyer passing by the scene said he saw the militants gathering around 20 youths from nearby to chant against the film. Within an hour or so, the assault began, guns blazing as the militants blasted into the compound."[19]

Whom to believe? Reuters' claim of a "spontaneous, unplanned public protest" over an anti-Muhammad film, or the AP's report that there was "no sign of a spontaneous protest" against the obscure movie?

THE *REAL* BENGHAZI HOAX

Did you know the Benghazi controversy is actually a made-up scandal, generated out of whole cloth by Republicans for partisan gain? This is the central theme of a recent e-book by David Brock, founder of the controversial, George Soros–funded, progressive activist organization Media Matters for America. Brock seems to believe it is illegitimate to ask questions about the State Department's repeated refusal to secure the U.S. special mission, the Obama administration's talking point fabrications, or why Special Forces were not deployed during the assault. These and other topics are deceptively dealt with in Brock's *The Benghazi Hoax*, coauthored with Media Matters executive Ari Rabin-Havt. I would not waste ink on Brock's fantastical farce except that some members of the news media actually took the e-book tripe seriously.

Brock is a known Hillary Clinton associate, so it's not surprising to read that he used the e-book to absolve Clinton of wrongdoing related to the September 11, 2012, attack. I invite Brock to review chapter 7 of this book, aptly titled, which thoroughly documents Clinton's central role in the Benghazi scandal. Progressive activist Brock further hails the State Department's Accountability Review Board report on Benghazi as thorough, fair, and accurate, despite its major reported flaws. "The Obama administration had done exactly what any citizen would expect of its government—investigated an overseas security breach in depth,"[21] Brock wrote. He praised ARB authors former ambassador Thomas Pickering and retired admiral Mike Mullen as "two figures with resumes beyond reproach."[22]

Brock, of course, did not report that Pickering has largely unreported ties to the revolutions in the Middle East and North Africa. Pickering is linked primarily through his role as a member of the small board of the International Crisis Group, or ICG, one of the main proponents of the international "Responsibility to Protect" doctrine.[23] The doctrine is the very military protocol used to justify the NATO bombing campaign that brought down Moammar Gaddafi's regime in Libya.

With no previous military, terrorism, or international news reporting experience to speak of, newfound national security expert Brock next disputed the claim that highly trained Special Forces were available and could have been deployed in time to make a difference in the September

11, 2012, attack. Brock may want to have a brief conversation with Martin Dempsey, chairman of the Joint Chiefs of Staff. We reported in chapter 3 that Dempsey admitted that highly trained Special Forces were stationed just a few hours away from Benghazi on the night of the attack but were not told to deploy. There are major questions about why this special force, known as the C-110 or the EUCOM CIF, was not immediately ordered to Libya, especially since the assumption for several hours that night was that our U.S. ambassador had been kidnapped.

Brock and cohort Rabin-Havt did not bother to raise the many questions prompted by Dempsey's testimony, including an admission to the highly unusual move of changing command of the Special Forces in the middle of the Benghazi attack. Instead, the dynamic Media Matters duo attempted to refute the exclusive Fox News interview discussed in chapter 3, in which an unnamed military special ops member, with face and voice disguised, contradicted Obama administration and ARB claims that there wasn't enough time for military forces to deploy the night of the attack. "It was a compelling argument, especially for a typical news consumer who possesses only a casual knowledge of military affairs," they wrote.[24]

"Military experts, however, dismissed these notions," they contend. The authors then quoted former defense secretary Robert Gates stating that the suggestion the military could have responded in time was based on "sort of a cartoonish impression of military capabilities and military forces."[25]

Brock and Rabin-Ravt further quoted former secretary of defense Leon Panetta arguing in February 2013 that a military response during the attack was unfeasible. Panetta told the Senate Armed Services Committee: "The reason simply is because armed UAVs, AC-130 gunships or fixed-wing fighters, with the associated tanking, you've got to provide air refueling abilities; you've got to arm all the weapons before you put them on the planes; targeting and support facilities, were not in the vicinity of Libya. And because of the distance, it would have taken at least nine to 12 hours, if not more, to deploy these forces to Benghazi."[26]

Brock and Rabin-Ravt entirely ignore the news-making remarks of Dempsey, who not only conceded that the C-110 Special Forces were stationed just a few hours away but also stated that command of the forces was transferred from the military's European command to AFRICOM, or the United States Africa Command, during the attack, a move that may warrant further investigation. Dempsey did not give any reason for the strange transfer of command, nor could he provide a timeline for the transfer the night of the attack.

Meanwhile, Brock and Rabin-Ravt seem to have been caught in a talking points scandal of their own. The industrious activists promote as fact the disputed claim that White House talking points on the Benghazi attack were edited to preserve a criminal investigation. Brock and Rabin-Havt do not cite any evidence for their claim about the talking points editing, and they fail to inform readers of the forty-six-page House Republican report that purports to have discovered another reason for scrubbing the talking points of references to terrorism: protecting the State Department's reputation (see chapter 8).[27] In other words, Brock and Rabin-Ravt are contradicted by lawmakers who had exclusive access to witnesses, classified documents, and intelligence reports.

Brock and Rabin-Ravt wrote of the talking points editing scandal:

> Over the next 24 hours, a set of talking points was drafted by the CIA's Office of Terrorism Analysis, and then altered multiple times through an interagency process involving the State Department, the White House, and others. In the end, much of the intelligence agency's specifics about the suspected perpetrators of the attack were removed in order to preserve the criminal investigation.[28]

The authors did not provide any reference for their claim. In fact, their sole argument rests on the integrity of then CIA director David Petraeus, who reportedly helped oversee the drafting of the talking-points document. "Petraeus would have had little to gain from misleading Congress, given both his track record of political independence and the enormous respect that he had from members of both parties," wrote Brock and Rabin-Havt.[29]

However, Petraeus might have had good reason to edit the talking points. As detailed in chapter 7, he was complicit with Hillary Clinton in advocating a plan to arm the Syrian rebels—a plan White House officials claim to have rejected.

It seems the real hoax perpetuated here is the publication of Brock's e-book, *The Benghazi Hoax.*

10

FROM BENGHAZI TO . . .
THE BOSTON BOMBING?

The real Benghazi story extends far beyond the deadly attacks on a U.S. special mission and CIA annex. We are today feeling the ramifications of the U.S.-coordinated arms shipments and vast supplies of aid and other support to the jihadist-led Mid-East rebels, with conflicts being fueled from Syria to Egypt to Israel to Mali to Algeria. Militants behind the Benghazi attacks may be linked to the Boston Marathon bombing and to the recent hijacking of an Algerian gas complex, targeting Westerners. In backing the rebels in Libya and later in Syria, the Obama administration may have unwittingly helped to create an al-Qaeda–allied army of thousands of highly motivated, well-trained gunmen. Besides wreaking havoc in the Middle East and Africa, these hard-line Islamists have been rampantly persecuting Middle Eastern and African Christians and other minorities. Among the ranks of these Islamists are Americans,

Australians, and Europeans who could return home to carry out domestic terrorist attacks.

Not only did we transfer weapons to the Mideastern rebels, it has been extensively reported that U.S. contractors working with the CIA have previously helped train the rebels fighting the regime of Syrian president Bashar al-Assad. Reuters reported that Obama allegedly signed a secret order in 2012 authorizing U.S. agencies such as the CIA to provide support to rebel forces in Syria.[1] Such support included helping run a secret military communications command center in Turkey while U.S. citizens were training rebels and possibly giving them equipment, at least since the summer of 2012.

The United States was behind covert training bases in Jordan and Turkey, where the Mideastern rebels were provided "two-week courses include training with Russian-designed 14.5-millimeter anti-tank rifles, anti-tank missiles, as well as 23-millimeter anti-aircraft weapons," according to the *LA Times*.[2] More than one year before other media outlets covered this story, I first documented the exact location of a U.S.-run training base for the Syrian rebels in the Jordanian town of Safawi in the country's northern desert region.[3] Three months later, I reported on growing collaboration between the Syrian opposition, including the U.S.-backed Free Syrian Army and al-Qaeda, as well as evidence the opposition was sending weapons to jihadists in Iraq.[4]

What did the Obama administration think would happen after it armed jihadists in Libya and then armed and trained Islamic gunmen fighting in Syria? Did the White House actually believe these battle-hardened, anti-Western extremists would simply forfeit their weapons when they were done fighting Assad or Muammar Gaddafi? I wish I could say we learned our lesson the hard way in Benghazi on September 12, 2012, when rebels we aided turned their weapons and ire on the United States. The Obama administration, however, evidenced little appreciation for national security, since it continued for more than a year to assist the anti-Assad rebels.

Just as alarming is a stream of reports about Westerners who joined the fight in Syria. Thomas Hegghammer, a Norwegian terrorism expert, penned an extensive article documenting that one in nine Westerners who joined these foreign jihadist insurgencies were complicit in terrorist plots back home.[5] While the figures are not exact, some estimates suggest Westerners fighting in Syria include 200 to 400 French citizens, 200 Germans, 200 to 300 Brits, 100 fighters from Belgium, and up to 200 or more from Australia. There have been reports of dozens of Americans conducting warfare alongside the rebels in Syria.[6]

WRECKING LIBYA, PROLIFERATING WEAPONS

Before we more directly address the global implications of our efforts to aid the rebels, efforts headquartered at the Benghazi mission and CIA annex until the attacks on our facilities there, let's take a brief look at how we essentially wrecked Libya by helping topple Gaddafi in hopes of bringing democracy to his country. Make no mistake about it: Gaddafi was a thug, a thief, and at times a terrorist supporter. He changed course somewhat after the U.S. invasion of Iraq, giving up his weapons of mass destruction, acceding to the Chemical Weapons Convention, and allowing the U.S. and international community to assist in the destruction of those weapons. The strongman, however, was far from a democratic leader. Still, Libyans were not living under the constant threat of radical Islamic factions during Gaddafi's rule. There were no reports of al-Qaeda erecting training camps in the country. Islamists were not waging war with the country's military while gaining swaths of territory where these thugs are imposing hard-line Sharia law.

A month before the 2012 terrorist attacks on our facilities in Benghazi, a Library of Congress report detailed how al-Qaeda had established a major base of operations in Libya in the aftermath of the U.S.–NATO campaign that deposed Gaddafi and his secular regime. The report, quoted in more depth earlier in this book, documented that al-Qaeda and affiliated organizations were not only establishing terrorist training camps but also enforcing Taliban-style Islamic law in Libya while the new, Western-backed Libyan government incorporated jihadists into its militias.[7]

As this book went to print, Islamists had seized three strategic Libyan ports and were tightening their grip on the south and east of the country amid fears that the weak, secular, Libyan government could lose total control. Just who are these Islamists who are now threatening to engulf the country? I'll let Reuters inform you. This one sentence in the news agency's March 6, 2014, report accurately sums up the devastating situation: "The weak government in Tripoli is struggling to control well-armed former anti-Gaddafi rebels and Islamist militias."[8] That's right. The rebels we helped arm in the name of democracy and freedom are currently the greatest threat to democracy and freedom in Libya.

It gets worse. A ninety-four-page United Nations report has warned that weapons initially sent to Benghazi are spreading from Libya to extremists at an "alarming rate," fueling conflicts from Gaza to Mali and beyond. The February 15, 2013, report authored by the UN Security Council's Group of Experts identified Libya as the key source of weapons transfers in the region, specifically blaming Qatar and the United Arab Emirates (UAE) for arming the rebels. While not referencing the U.S. support for the arms transfers, the UN experts said they had found that Qatar and the UAE had breached the arms embargo on Libya during the 2011 uprising by arming the rebels. The experts said Qatar had denied the accusation, while the UAE had not responded.[9] As we documented in chapter 2, the Obama administration used Qatar and the UAE as cutouts to ship weapons to the Libyan and later Syrian rebels. The *New York Times* reported that after discussions among members of the National Security Council, the Obama administration backed arms shipments to Libyan rebels from both Qatar and the UAE.[10]

In its devastating report, the UN cites cases, both proven and under investigation, of illicit transfers from Libya to more than twelve countries and also to terror and criminal groups, including heavy and light weapons; man-portable air-defence systems, or MANPADS; small arms and related ammunition; and explosives and mines.[11] The report failed to mention the key involvement of the Obama administration, as described in mainstream media reports, in coordinating the Arab arms shipments to the rebels.

"NIGHTMARE" THREAT TO AIRLINERS WORLDWIDE

The proliferation of MANPADS in Libya is now one of the greatest threats to airliners around the world. Recall from previous chapters that thousands of MANPADS were looted when Gaddafi's reserves were unprotected following the NATO campaign there in 2011. The U.S. special mission in Benghazi was desperately attempting to retake the antiaircraft weapons, with reports that hundreds of missiles were tracked going to the group Al-Qaeda in the Islamic Maghreb (AQIM), the al-Qaeda franchise based in Algeria that is now considered one of the gravest threats to the United States. Thousands more fell into the hands of assorted other jihad groups.

Former CIA director David Petraeus has warned of a "nightmare" scenario in which missile proliferation could provide terrorists the capability to shoot down a civilian airliner, an ironic turn of events since Petraeus himself was one of the driving forces behind arming the Libyan revels and toppling Gaddafi. Speaking about the MANPAD proliferation, Petraeus stated, "As you know, that was always our worst nightmare, that a civilian airliner would be shot down by one. Which is why we were so concerned when they moved around."[12]

The antiaircraft threat combined with our meddling in the Syrian insurgency may have already precipitated the unprecedented, nearly weeklong closure of twenty-two U.S. embassies in the summer of 2014. At the time it was reported the closures were in response to an intercepted message from al-Qaeda operatives in Yemen. I reported the threat was the direct result of U.S.-supported efforts under way to purge al-Qaeda affiliates from the ranks of the Syrian rebels.[13]

The Western support for the jihadist Libyan and Syria rebels, a policy that helped create an al-Qaeda–linked army, may have emboldened the jihadists behind the brazen assault on an Algerian gas complex in January 2013, where foreigners, including Americans, were employed. In the Algerian assault, Al-Qaeda in the Islamic Maghreb laid siege for four days to the gas complex, with the ordeal finally ending in the deaths of thirty-eight hostages and twenty-nine kidnappers after Algerian forces stormed the compound. A senior Algerian official was quoted in the *New York Times* saying several Egyptian members of the group behind the bloody gas complex siege also took part in the Benghazi assaults.[14] The Algerian official said that information was extracted during the interrogations of the jihadists who had survived the compound assault. American counterterrorism and intelligence officials told the *Times* that Ansar al-Sharia, the group that carried out the attack on the diplomatic mission in Benghazi, had connections to Al-Qaeda in the

Islamic Maghreb. I cannot repeat enough that an arm of Ansar, the February 17 Martyrs Brigade, served as the quick reaction force inside the U.S. Benghazi mission, hired by the State Department while top officials working under Hillary Clinton nixed a team of U.S. special forces and repeatedly rejected military overtures for more security.

CNN reported that three men who participated in the Benghazi assaults with Ansar al-Sharia were later traced by counterterrorism officials to northern Mali, where they are believed to have connected with the jihad organization led by Mokhtar Belmokhtar. It was Belmokhtar's group that claimed responsibility for the Algerian gas facility siege. Another intelligence source told CNN that Belmokhtar had received a call in the immediate aftermath of the Benghazi attack from someone in or close to the city. The person on the other end of the call stated, "Mabruk! Mabruk!" meaning "Congratulations" in Arabic, according to the source.[15]

BOSTON BOMBING

Militants linked to the Western-backed Libyan rebels have some ties to the April 15, 2013, Boston Marathon bombing in which two pressure cooker bombs exploded, killing 3 people and injuring more than 260. The common thread runs through al-Qaeda in the Arabian Peninsula (AQAP), one of the deadliest members of the al-Qaeda conglomerate. AQAP previously attempted several major attacks within the United States.

The group was the first al-Qaeda member to comment on

the Benghazi attack, releasing a statement arguing the assaults on the U.S. mission and nearby CIA annex were revenge for the death of Abu Yahya al-Libi, one of the most senior al-Qaeda operatives. AQAP did not directly claim responsibility for the Benghazi attacks. Al-Libi, of Libyan descent, was killed in a U.S. drone strike in Pakistan in June 2012.

Lost in the news media coverage about the U.S. response to the Libya attacks was that one day before the assaults, on September 10, 2012, al-Qaeda leader Ayman al-Zawahiri released a forty-two-minute video announcing al-Libi's death. Released on a jihadi online forum fewer than eighteen hours before the Benghazi attack, Zawahiri urged jihadists, and particularly those in Libya, to avenge the killing of al-Libi. "His blood urges you and incites you to fight and kill the crusaders," he said.[16]

CNN quoted sources disclosing that several Yemeni men belonging to AQAP took part in the Benghazi attacks. One senior U.S. law enforcement official told CNN that "three or four members of al-Qaida in the Arabian Peninsula" took part in the attack. Another source quoted by CNN as being briefed on the Benghazi investigation said Western intelligence services "suspect the men may have been sent by the group specifically to carry out the attack. But it's not been ruled out that they were already in the city and participated as the opportunity arose," continued the CNN report.[17]

AQAP has also been tied to the Boston bombing. The jihadi group is behind *Inspire* magazine, the periodical thought to have provided bomb-building instructions for

Tamerlan and Dzhokhar Tsarnaev, the accused Boston Marathon terrorists.

AQAP has previously attempted attacks on U.S. soil. One such attempt was the 2009 Christmas Day plot by a Nigerian recruited by the group to blow up a plane flying into Detroit. That attack failed when the suspect's device malfunctioned. In October 2010, AQAP reportedly attempted to blow up planes destined for the United States using printer bombs disguised as air cargo. The plan was thwarted after a tip from Saudi intelligence. In April 2012 it was reported that a British informant working for Saudi counterterrorism thwarted an AQAP plot to bomb a U.S-bound airliner.[18]

U.S.-AIDED REBELS PERSECUTE CHRISTIANS, MODERATE MUSLIMS

U.S. support for the Libyan and Syrian rebels has undoubtedly resulted in widespread reports of the persecution of moderate Muslims, Christians, and others targeted by gunmen enforcing hard-line Sharia Islamic law. The civilized world was in shock in February 2014 when an extremist group in the rebel stronghold of Aleppo in Syria's north live-tweeted the amputation of a hand. The group tweeted that the blindfolded man being punished was a thief who had asked to have his hand severed "in order to cleanse his sins."[19]

One of the main organizations originally armed by the United States was the Free Syrian Army (FSA), with reports of arms shipments from Libya to FSA bases in Turkey. The FSA is one of the main organized armed opposition structures fighting Assad. The U.S. aid to the FSA came amid scores of reports worldwide that al-Qaeda and other jihad groups are among the ranks of the Free Syrian Army.

The FSA has been widely accused of imposing Sharia law while its gunmen have been caught targeting minorities. The *Huffington Post* detailed that the U.S.-supported FSA has created a "Sharia law enforcement police force" in secular Syria "that is a replica of the Wahhabi police in Saudi Arabia—forcing ordinary citizens to abide by the Sharia code." According to the *Post*, Syria has never known Sharia law.[20]

Christians in Syria say they are being threatened by FSA branches. Churches have been attacked. Christian leaders say they feel threatened. The Vatican news agency Agenzia Fides reported that 90 percent of the Christian population of Homs—about ten thousand people—were expelled from their homes by members of the FSA's Faruq Brigade. The agency quoted Orthodox Metropolitan sources saying the FSA militants went door-to-door in the neighborhoods of Hamidiya and Bustan al-Diwan, forcing Christians to flee without giving them the chance to take their belongings.[21]

Christians in Libya are not faring well, either. In February 2014 Libyan police found seven Coptic Christians shot execution-style on a beach in eastern Libya, the second such killing targeting Christians that year. About 5 percent of Libya, or three hundred thousand Libyans, are Coptic Christians. Those Christians may soon find themselves living officially under Islamic law. As I was finishing this chapter, Libya's national assembly voted to make Sharia the basis for the country's law, with a statement declaring that "Islamic law is the source of legislation in Libya . . . All state institutions need to comply with this."[22]

APPENDIX A

LIES AND MISLEADING CLAIMS

Ever since the September 11, 2012, Benghazi attacks, the Obama administration has done everything it can to cover up the truth. I've exposed these lies and misleading claims in detail throughout the book. Here is a snapshot look at all the various falsehoods that have been told by those responsible and their lackeys.

LIES

United Nations ambassador Susan Rice on September 16, 2012, visited five morning television programs to offer the official Obama administration response to the Benghazi attacks. In nearly identical statements, Rice asserted that the attacks were a spontaneous protest in response to a "hateful video."

Four days after Rice's disinformation, Obama himself was questioned on September 20, 2012, about whether the Benghazi attack was carried out by terrorists. He responded, "What we do know is that the natural protests that arose because of the outrage over the video were used as an excuse by extremists to see if they can also directly harm U.S. interests." He was pressed at a town hall event hosted by Univision about whether al-Qaeda was behind the assault. He replied, "Well, we don't know yet."[1]

Numerous other Obama administration officials, including then secretary of state Hillary Clinton and others, claimed the attacks were in response to the obscure anti-Islam film while they minimized terrorism. Obama and Clinton appeared in an ad campaign denouncing the anti-Muhammad film. The ads reportedly aired on seven Pakistani networks.

These assertions are contradicted by logic, surveillance video, and testimony from those who were on the ground during the assaults who described a coordinated attack by jihadists.

One day before Rice made the morning show rounds, CIA officials received an e-mail from the CIA's Libya station chief stating the attacks were "not an escalation of protests."[2] Gregory Hicks, the No. 2 U.S. official in Libya at the time of the September 11, 2012, attacks, testified that he knew immediately the attacks were terror strikes, not a protest turned violent. According to Hicks, "everybody in the mission" believed it was an act of terror "from the get-go."

The day after the attack, Libya's deputy ambassador to London, Ahmad Jibril, told the BBC that Ansar al-Sharia carried out the assault.[3]

Libyan President Mohammed el-Megarif was even more direct, saying foreigner jihadists who infiltrated Libya planned the attack and used some local Libyans during the event. He called the idea "that this criminal and cowardly act was a spontaneous protest that just spun out of control is completely unfounded and preposterous." The Libyan president said, "We firmly believe that this was a precalculated, preplanned attack that was carried out specifically to attack the U.S. Consulate."[4]

The claim of a spontaneous protest is further contradicted by logic. Spontaneous protesters usually do not usually show up with weapons, erect armed checkpoints surrounding a foreign compound, and have insider knowledge of the facility while deploying military-style tactics to storm a U.S. mission.

It is further difficult to believe spontaneous protesters know the exact location of a secretive CIA annex, including the specific coordinates of a building that were likely utilized to launch precision mortar strikes. To believe the spontaneous protesters narrative, one must then accept that such protesters were capable of mounting a fierce, hours-long gun battle with U.S. forces stationed inside the CIA annex.

LIES

In Susan Rice's initial Sunday show remarks on September 16, she told ABC News, "We believe that folks in Benghazi, a small number of people came to the embassy—or to the consulate, rather, to replicate the sort of challenge that was posed in Cairo."[5]

Secretary of State Hillary Clinton used the word "consulate" several times during her testimony on Benghazi.

While many in the government have been careful not to use the word "consulate" in describing the U.S. facility attacked in Benghazi, some administration officials have indeed called the assaulted building a "consulate." Government documents from the State Department's ARB report into congressional and senatorial investigations of documents released by the State Department, White House, Pentagon, and Intelligence Community carefully label the facility a "U.S. Special Mission" and not a "consulate." In fact, the ARB divulges that the mission was so special it possessed a "non-status" making security provisions to the facility difficult. The ARB also relates a decision "to treat Benghazi as a temporary, residential facility."

LIES

The administration has claimed the Benghazi attacks were an extension of protests outside the U.S. embassy in Cairo, Egypt, that same day. We were told the Cairo protests were also about the anti-Islam film.

The protests were actually announced days in advance as part of a movement to free the so-called blind sheikh, Omar Abdel-Rahman, who is serving a life sentence in the United States for conspiracy in the 1993 World Trade Center bombing. In July 2012, Rahman's son, Abdallah Abdel Rahman, threatened to organize a protest at the U.S. embassy in Cairo and detain the employees inside.[6] In fact, on the day of the September 11, 2012, protests in Cairo, CNN's Nic Robertson interviewed Rahman's son, who described the protest as being about freeing his father. No Muhammad film was mentioned. A big banner calling for Rahman's release can be seen as Robertson walked to the embassy protests.[7]

LIES

Mike Morell, then acting CIA director, claimed references to terrorism were scrubbed from the White House talking points "to prevent compromising an ongoing criminal investigation" of the attack on the U.S. mission.

A Republican House Interim Progress Report on the events in Benghazi relates that lawmakers who penned the investigation were given access to classified e-mails and other communications that prove the talking points were not edited to protect classified information but instead to protect the State Department's reputation, directly contradicting Morell's claims.[9]

LIES

The State Department's ARB report claims the armed February 17 Martyrs Brigade members hired to protect the U.S. special mission actually helped American personnel escape a roadblock when the compound came under attack. It paints a picture of Brigade members as helpful to American personnel during the attack.

A Senate report reveals the February 17 Martyrs Brigade militia refused to "provide cover" for the U.S. security team that was trapped inside the compound. Relates the report: "Outside the compound, the security team asked February 17 Martyrs Brigade members to 'provide cover' for them to advance to the gate of the Temporary Mission Facility with gun trucks. The February Brigade members refused, saying they preferred to negotiate with the attackers instead."[10]

LIES

The State Department's ARB report states security personnel inside the U.S. Benghazi compound were armed, even describing how the security officers retrieved their weapons.[11]

Representative Westmoreland, chairman of the House Intelligence Subcommittee, told Fox News that State Department employees inside the mission "were not armed, not kitted up and there hadn't been any shots fired from our side as far as the testimony reveals." Westmoreland was commenting on closed-door testimony given to his intelligence committee.[12] In another interview with Fox News, Westmoreland stated that one of the U.S. security officers was barefoot during the attack, while another two were "riding around in a Land Cruiser."[13] If the witness testimony of unarmed security officers is accurate, it would mean the ARB details were fabricated out of whole cloth.

LIES

For months, Obama administration officials repeatedly denied supplying arms to rebels fighting the insurgency against Syrian president Bashar al-Assad amid reports the arms pipeline may have originated in part in Libya.

According to the *New York Times*, the CIA started helping Arab governments and Turkey to obtain and ship weapons to the rebels fighting the regime of Syrian president Bashar al-Assad. The *Times* reported this covert aid to the Syrian rebels started in early 2012.[14] The *Times* later reported that the weapons airlifts to Syria began on a small scale and continued intermittently through the fall of 2012, expanding into a steady and much heavier flow later that year.[15] (My own sources say the airlifts started several months before fall 2012.)

LIES

Multiple administration and Pentagon officials claimed they thought the attack in Benghazi was over after the initial assault, so therefore a rescue mission or air support would not have made a difference.

How could the Obama administration have known what the gunmen had planned or that the first wave was the only attack to be carried out? Second, witnesses on the ground, including CIA contractors who were inside the annex, said there was no lull in the fighting at all.[16]

LIES

Martin Dempsey, chairman of the Joint Chiefs of Staff, claimed there was not enough time for C-110 Special Forces to have made it to Benghazi from their temporary station base in Croatia. Dempsey was asked whether he agreed with a Fox News timeline that the C-110 could deploy in four to six hours. "No, I would not agree to that timeline," he stated. "The travel time alone would have been more than that, and that is if they were sitting on the tarmac."[17]

Dempsey's remarks are inaccurate. Even a large passenger jet can travel from the farthest point of Croatia to Benghazi in about two and a half hours or less.

LIES

Clearly denying any existence of an order to wait or stand down, the State Department's ARB says a response team one mile away in the CIA annex was "not delayed by orders from superiors."[18] Multiple Obama administration officials claimed rescue teams were not delayed by any orders.

CIA agents on the ground in Benghazi testified to lawmakers that they were loaded into vehicles and ready to aid the besieged U.S. special mission on September 11, 2012, but were told by superiors to "wait." Representative Westmoreland, who again is head of the House intelligence subcommittee that interviewed the CIA employees, explained that while there was no "stand-down order," there was a disagreement at the nearby CIA annex about how quickly to respond. Westmoreland revealed that some CIA agents wanted to storm the Benghazi compound immediately, but they were told to wait while the agency collected intelligence on the ongoing attack.[19]

LIES

The State Department's ARB report claims "civilians" who were likely "good Samaritans" found Ambassador Chris Stevens' body and transported him to the Benghazi Medical Center.

If this narrative is accurate, then we must believe that "good Samaritans" carrying the body of the most high-profile American in Libya made it past heavy roadblocks established by armed militants around the periphery of the U.S. compound.

LIES

Hillary Clinton testified on January 23, 2013, that no one within the government ever recommended the closure of the U.S. facility in Benghazi.[20]

Clinton's testimony is contradicted by Lt. Col. Andrew Wood, who led the U.S. military's efforts to supplement diplomatic security in Libya. Wood testified that he personally recommended the Benghazi mission be closed on security grounds.[21]

AND MORE LIES

During her Benghazi testimony, Clinton implied that she didn't know about the procurement or transfer of weapons out of Libya to Turkey.

Clinton, it seems, was not only personally involved in the arms-to–Syrian jihadists scheme; she was reportedly a ringleader. The *New York Times* described Clinton as one of the driving forces behind advocating a plan to arm the Syrian rebels.[22]

APPENDIX B

QUESTIONS FOR THE HOUSE SELECT COMMITTEE ON BENGHAZI

The following is a list of suggested questions, based largely on the information documented in this book, for the House Select Committee on Benghazi to ask to members and former members of the Obama administration. Included are specific questions to be posed to former secretary of state Hillary Clinton.

SECURITY

- An eighty-five-page Senate report concluded that, according to the State Department, the Benghazi "Mission facility did not store classified information, and therefore no Marine contingent was present."[1] What then was the purpose of the U.S. special mission? What kinds of activities transpired at the mission? This is one of the most important questions that must be asked.

- A top official revealed the State Department refused a request to install guard towers at the doomed U.S. facility in Benghazi (*see chapter 1*). Why were the guard towers not installed? One reason initially provided is that the towers would attract too much attention to the facility. Why was the State Department so concerned about attracting too much attention to this particular facility? Other nations had a public presence in Benghazi.

- In an interview with CNN on November 18, 2013, Rep. Lynn Westmoreland (R-GA), chairman of the House Intelligence Subcommittee on Oversight and Investigations, disclosed that his committee had learned a directive was issued August 11—one month before the attack—telling Benghazi staff they were on their own.[2] Is this accurate? If so, who issued this directive?

- The mission's entire external security depended on "unarmed, locally contracted Blue Mountain Libya guards," the State-sponsored Accountability Review Board (ARB) report relates.[3] Why were unarmed guards protecting a U.S. compound in one of the most dangerous cities in Libya?

- Another critical question: Why was internal security for the compound—the quick reaction force—provided by armed members of the February 17 Martyrs Brigade? The February 17 Brigade is part of the al-Qaeda–linked Ansar al-Sharia, a militia that advocates the strict implementation of Islamic law and that took credit for previous attacks against other diplomatic posts in Benghazi before the September 11 attacks. Ultimately, Ansar al-Sharia was implicated in the Benghazi attacks, as well. How could the State Department trust an al-Qaeda–tied Islamic extremist militia to serve as the armed quick reaction force within the U.S. special mission? Who within the State Department approved the February 17 Brigade force?

- According to the ARB report, the attackers appear to have used fuel that was stored next to uninstalled generators at the February 17 Martyrs Brigade living quarters to burn that building.[4] Is there information indicating that the February 17 Brigade militia deliberately left the fuel cans there?

- The intruders were said to have inside knowledge of the layout of the compound, including the precise location of a secret safe room where Ambassador Chris Stevens was holed up. Is there information indicating that the February 17 Brigade militia provided the attackers with critical insider information? Were the militia members, and perhaps former guards at the compound, among the gunmen who carried out the actual assault that night?

- Libyan warlord Abdul Basit Haroun divulged to Reuters that he is behind some of the biggest shipments of weapons from Libya to Syria. Most of the weapons were sent to Turkey, he said, where they were in turn smuggled into neighboring Syria.[5] Haroun was reportedly a former member of the February 17 Brigade militia. Did the militia aid the United States in procuring weapons for Mideast rebels? Is this why the militia worked from within the U.S. special mission?

- In the months before the September 11, 2012, assault, the State Department pulled government Security Support Teams (SSTs), special U.S. forces trained for counterattacks on U.S. embassies or threats against diplomatic personnel. Why were these forces removed? Even after their removal, why wasn't an SST temporarily redeployed to Libya ahead of the 9/11 anniversary to beef up security on the one day jihadists are known to be more motivated to attack?

- The State Department denied a request for the continued use of an aircraft to move personnel and security equipment in Libya. Such an aircraft could have aided in the evacuation of the victims after the attack. Ultimately, the U.S. special mission had to wait for a Libyan C-130 transport cargo aircraft and other planes to be secured to move the victims from Benghazi to Tripoli and then from Tripoli to Western hospitals. Who pulled the aircraft? Why was it removed?

- One month before the September 11, 2012, attack, a fifty-four-page Library of Congress report warned of al-Qaeda's increasing presence in Libya, including inside Benghazi. What additional security precautions, if any, were taken in light of this alarming information?

- Key Pentagon officials, including the commander of U.S. forces in Africa, were not aware of the existence of the CIA annex that operated 1.2 miles away from the Benghazi mission and was the second target on the night of the attacks (*see chapter 1*). Why were these officials not briefed on the mission's whereabouts and existence? How could the military protect the facility when top Pentagon brass, including Gen. Carter Ham, then commander of U.S. Africa Command, did not even know it existed?

- The State Department labeled the attacked Benghazi facility a "U.S. special mission." Why was it given such an unusual designation?

SECRETIVE ACTIVITIES

- Were the U.S. special mission and/or the nearby CIA annex in Benghazi involved in any way in procuring and shipping weapons to the jihadist rebels fighting the regime of Bashar al-Assad of Syria or to any other rebels fighting in the Middle East or Africa?

- Ambassador Chris Stevens' original role in Libya was to serve as the main interlocutor between the Obama administration and the rebels based in Benghazi. Was Stevens himself involved in recruiting and/or vetting jihadists or coordinating arms shipments to the gunmen fighting Assad's regime in Syria or to any other rebels fighting in the Middle East or Africa?

- The *New York Times* reported that from offices at "secret locations," American intelligence officers "helped the Arab governments shop for weapons" and vet rebel commanders and groups "to determine who should receive the weapons as they arrive." The CIA declined to comment to the *Times* on the shipments to Syria or its role in them.[6] Where were these purported secret offices located? Was this a reference to the secret CIA annex and obscure U.S. special mission in Benghazi where Stevens held his final meeting with a Turkish diplomat?

- *The New York Times* reported in December 2012 that Stevens himself facilitated an application to the State Department for the sale of weapons, filed by one Marc Turi, whom the *Times* describes as an "American arms merchant who had sought to provide weapons to Libya."[7] Why was Stevens aiding in an application for an arms merchant? Is this an ordinary activity for a U.S. ambassador? Was Stevens involved in activities in Libya beyond the diplomatic realm? If so, could these activities have any relation to the Benghazi attacks?

- Fox News reported that Stevens was in Benghazi the very night of the attacks "to negotiate a weapons transfer in an effort to get SA-7 missiles out of the hands of Libya-based extremists."[8] Is this accurate?

- In August 2013 there was speculation on Capitol Hill that U.S. agencies operating in Benghazi "were secretly helping to move surface-to-air missiles out of Libya, through Turkey, and into the hands of Syrian rebels."[9] Were these activities indeed taking place? Were such activities transpiring in the U.S. facilities in Benghazi? Could it be that the movement of these weapons provoked the Benghazi attacks?

- The *New York Times* reported that U.S. intelligence officers aided Arab governments in obtaining weapons, "including a large procurement from Croatia."[10] The C-110 forty-man special ops force was reportedly "training" in Croatia during the Benghazi attacks. The force was not deployed to help the embattled Benghazi facilities. Was the C-110 in Croatia to protect, collect, or ship the weapons reportedly procured in that country?

NO REINFORCEMENTS

- The ARB report provided a timeline of the attacks, an accounting adopted by the Obama administration. The report claims the initial assault on the U.S. special mission in Benghazi started between 9:45 p.m. and 10:00 p.m. local time and lasted until about midnight, when all but two Americans were evacuated to the CIA annex about a mile away. According to the ARB report, at midnight the annex was attacked intermittently for an hour by gunfire and RPGs. The ARB report claims the next phase of the attack started at about 5:15 a.m. local time, describing the second wave of attacks as consisting of heavy mortar and RPG assaults.[11]

- However, witnesses on the ground, including CIA contractors inside the annex, said there was no lull in the fighting at all.[12] The "lull" claim is central to the Obama administration's explanation for why no air support or special forces were deployed to Benghazi. Was there a lull or not? If not, why didn't the Obama administration immediately deploy reinforcements? If there was no lull, why did the State Department claim there was?

- Why were no reinforcements sent the night of the attacks? The government's standard response is patently absurd. They say they thought the attack was over following the initial assault, so therefore there was just not enough time to send a rescue mission or air support. But how could they have known what the gunmen had planned or that the "first wave" was the only attack to be carried out?

- After the initial assault Stevens went missing. As reported, the acting assumption of the decision makers that night was that Stevens had been kidnapped. Why were special forces not immediately deployed for a potential hostage situation involving a supposedly kidnapped U.S. ambassador?

- On the night of the attack, Gen. Carter Ham was placed in charge of the C-110 special ops force maintained for rapid response to emergencies. The force exists for the very purpose of responding to events such as the Benghazi attacks. Why was command of the C-110 transferred from the military's European command to Ham's Africa Command in the middle of the attack?

- Instead of deploying to Libya from their "training" position in Croatia, the C-110 were reportedly told on the night of the Benghazi attacks to begin preparations to return to their normal operating base in Germany. Why was this order given? Why was a special force that exists for the very purpose of an emergency like Benghazi told in the middle of a massive attack on our U.S. mission to return to their normal operating base?

- Former deputy Libyan ambassador and whistle-blower Gregory Hicks said he contacted AFR-ICOM the night of the attack but received no support.[13] What justified the lack of support?

- Representative Westmoreland, chairman of the House Intelligence Subcommittee, commenting on closed-door testimony given to his intelligence committee, told Fox News in November 2013 that State Department employees inside the mission "were not armed, not kitted up and there hadn't been any shots fired from our side as far as the testimony reveals."[14] In another interview with Fox News that same month, Westmoreland further stated one of the U.S. security officers was barefoot during the attack while another two were "riding around in a Land Cruiser."[15] This witness testimony of unarmed personnel directly contradicts the narrative in the ARB report, which specifically claims the personnel inside the compound were armed. The document even describes how the security officers retrieved their weapons.[16] How does the State Department explain these glaring contradictions?

- U.S. government agencies, including the CIA, have long denied the persistent claim that there was a "stand down" order during the attack. However, CIA agents on the ground in Benghazi testified to lawmakers that they were loaded into vehicles and ready to aid the besieged U.S. special mission on September 11, 2012, but were told by superiors to wait.[17] Were any U.S. personnel ready to mount a rescue operation told to wait? If so, this would further contradict claims made by the State Department's ARB report, which states that the response team one mile away in the CIA annex was "not delayed by orders from superiors."[18] How does the State Department explain this discrepancy?

- It is known that the Libyan rebels looted Muammar Gaddafi's reserves of man-portable air-defense systems, or MANPADS. Were the antiaircraft missiles in the hands of the Libyan rebels or other jihadists a major threat that impeded the possibility of dispatching U.S. aircraft to aid the American targets during the Benghazi attack? Was the MANPAD proliferation taken into consideration when deciding whether to send air support to Benghazi?

AMBASSADOR STEVENS

- Was Stevens or his body held hostage at any point. If so, by whom? How was Stevens' corpse eventually released? Were there negotiations to secure the remains? What promises did we make for Stevens' body, and to whom? If Stevens' body were held hostage, why do we not know about it?

- Thomas Pickering, the State Department's lead Benghazi investigator and author of the State-sponsored Accountability Review Board report, raised some eyebrows when he refused to deny there was a plan to kidnap Stevens. The response took place at a House Oversight and Government Reform committee hearing on Benghazi in mid-September 2013, when Rep. Cynthia Lummis (R-WY), asked Pickering directly about a potential kidnapping plot. Is any U.S. agency in possession of intelligence indicating that the Benghazi attack was a kidnap operation gone awry? Was there a plan to kidnap Stevens and hold him for the exchange of high-level prisoners?

- Abdallah Dhu al-Bajadin, who was identified by U.S. officials as a known weapons experts for al-Qaeda, wrote on a jihadi website that Stevens was killed by lethal injection after plans to kidnap him during the Benghazi assault went awry. Obviously we need to take anything a terrorist says with more than a grain of salt. However, is there any information that would indicate Stevens was killed by lethal injection? Was a full autopsy performed? If so, why haven't the results been made public? Were any toxins found in Stevens' blood?

- The ARB report states the intruders smoked up Villa C, likely to make breathing so difficult that anyone inside the safe room would need to come out. And that seems to be just what happened. According to the ARB report, Stevens and his guards had no choice but to exit the safe room for fresh air. How did Stevens and his guards make it from the safe room, where they were being smoked out, into a bathroom in the Villa without any of the intruders noticing?

- An Obama administration e-mail released in May 2014 states that in the immediate aftermath of the Benghazi attacks, someone at a local Libyan hospital called to report Stevens was at the medical center and was "alive and well." The e-mail entirely contradicts the ARB report, which states the caller at the hospital said a man matching Stevens' description was brought to the medical center and was "unresponsive." How does the State Department explain this discrepancy? Was the hospitalized ambassador alive and well, or unresponsive? If Stevens was alive and well, as the Obama administration e-mail claims, then how did he die?

- How did Stevens' body get from a heavily besieged compound to the Benghazi Medical Center? The ARB report says Stevens was transported by "good Samaritans."[19] How did these "good Samaritans" make it past Ansar al-Sharia roadblocks with the body of the most high-profile American in Libya? And just who are these "good Samaritans" in Benghazi who risked their lives to make it through the various checkpoints all the way to the hospital?

- The Benghazi Medical Center was controlled by the rebels. The ARB report called the facility "dangerous for American personnel" because of Ansar Al-Sharia's known presence inside the hospital.[20] Did Ansar or any other Islamic extremist group become aware of Stevens' presence at the hospital?

- The ARB report explains that the "presumed remains of Ambassador Stevens" were brought to the airport by Libyan contacts in "a local ambulance at 0825 local, and the TDY RSO verified Ambassador Stevens' identity."[21] The ARB report does not explain how these "Libyan contacts" managed to get Stevens' body out of the "dangerous" hospital. Who were the Libyan contacts?

- The eighty-five-page Senate report reveals details about how Stevens' body arrived at the tarmac with the waiting evacuation airplane. "After more than three hours of negotiations and communications with Libyan officials who expressed concern about the security situation at the hospital, the Libyan government arranged for the Libyan Shield Militia to provide transportation and an armed escort from the airport."[22] Who was holding Stevens' body, and how were the remains eventually released? Were any promises made by the U.S. government for the release of the body?

MUSLIM BROTHERHOOD CONNECTION

- Are any of the attackers tied to Egyptian former president Mohamed Morsi or any other Muslim Brotherhood figures?

- It is known that the U.S. government had knowledge indicating some Egyptian participation in the assault. Why did the Obama administration initially keep this critical piece of information from the public?

- Unsubstantiated Arabic-language reports from the Middle East claim a passport belonging to the alleged killer of Stevens had been recovered at the home of Egyptian Muslim Brotherhood deputy leader Khairat el-Shater. Is this true? Sens. John McCain (R-AZ) and Lindsey Graham (R-SC) reportedly visited el-Shater in prison in August 2013, spending over an hour talking to the Brotherhood leader.[23] What did the senators discuss with el-Shater?

- The White House sought at first to connect the September 11, 2012, Benghazi attack to protests that same day in Cairo, Egypt, in which rioters climbed the walls of the U.S. embassy and tore down the American flag. Those Cairo protests were widely reported to be acts of defiance against an anti-Muhammad movie. However, the protests were actually announced days in advance as part of a movement to free the so-called blind sheikh, Omar Abdel-Rahman, who is serving a life sentence in the United States for his role in the 1993 World Trade Center bombing. Is there information suggesting any of the Benghazi attackers were motivated by the campaign to release Rahman?

- There were unconfirmed reports that Egypt's former Morsi government would not allow the U.S. officials to interrogate suspects in the attack. Is this accurate?

- On September 10, 2012, one day before the Benghazi assaults, al-Qaeda leader Ayman al-Zawahiri released a video calling for attacks on Americans in Libya to avenge the death of Abu Yahya al-Libi, one of the most senior al-Qaeda operatives, who was killed by a U.S. drone strike. Is there information indicating the attackers were sent by Zawahiri or were part of an effort to avenge al-Libi's elimination?

- Is there information indicating Iran or any other state actor was in any way involved in the Benghazi attacks?

- In October 2013 US Special Forces seized wanted militant Abu Anas al-Libi, who was living openly in his home in Libya, in a daylight raid outside his home while his family looked on. Family members immediately and predictably told the news media about the raid, which thwarted an ongoing operation in which covert U.S. operatives were hours from arresting Ahmed Abu Khattala, a senior leader of the Ansar al-Sharia militia wanted for the Benghazi attack. Why was al-Libi seized in a public operation in Tripoli?

- Obama previously vowed to make it a "priority" to bring the Benghazi suspects "to justice." Did he personally make the call to arrest al-Libi before Khattala, and to do so in such a public manner?

QUESTIONS FOR HILLARY CLINTON

- Because the U.S. Benghazi facility was so dangerous and did not meet the security standards set by the State Department, the Benghazi mission actually required special waivers in order to be occupied by American personnel. Such a waiver could have only been issued by you, Madam Secretary. Did you issue this waiver? If so, were you adequately briefed on the glaring security lapses at the facility?

- If you were not fully briefed, how can you justify issuing this waiver? (Some of the necessary waivers the Senate affirmed could have been issued at lower levels within the State Department. However, other departures, such as the co-location requirement, could only be approved by the Secretary of State.[24] The co-location requirement refers to an unusual housing setup in Benghazi where intelligence and State Department personnel were kept in two separate locations.)

- The decisions to deny guard towers and to pull a special reaction team from the hot zone of Libya were made by your top deputies. We know you took particular interest in Libya, the lynchpin for the so-called Arab Spring. Were you aware of these and other perplexing security decisions made by your deputies regarding the Benghazi compound?

- Not only were your deputies the ones who made central perplexing security decisions; they were also involved in drafting the now-discredited talking points on the Benghazi attacks. Were you involved with the talking points drafting?

- Did you know the attacks were coordinated jihadist assaults when you publicly blamed the attacks on an obscure YouTube video?

- On January 23, 2013, you testified under oath that no one within the government ever recommended the closure of the U.S. facilities in the Libyan city. Your testimony is contradicted by Lt. Col. Andrew Wood, who led the U.S. military's efforts to supplement diplomatic security in Libya. Wood testified that he personally recommended the Benghazi mission be closed. Did you mislead lawmakers and the public under oath?

- According to congressional testimony by Gregory Hicks, the former State Department deputy chief of mission and chargé d'affairs, who was in Libya at the time of the attack, Stevens went to the compound that day in part because you wanted to convert the shanty complex into a permanent mission as a symbol of the new Libya. Hicks said you wanted to announce the establishment of a permanent U.S. State Department facility during your planned visit there in December 2012. Apparently Stevens was up against a specific, tight funding deadline to complete an extensive survey of the mission so the compound could be converted. Did you play any role in Stevens' decision to go to the dangerous facility on the anniversary of the 9/11 terrorist attacks, a day when jihadists are particularly motivated to strike our country's assets?

- You should have been aware of the terrorist camps in Benghazi. Fox News reported that the officials at the U.S. mission in Benghazi convened an "emergency meeting" in August 2012 to discuss the training camps. The news network obtained a government cable addressed to your office stating that the U.S. diplomats in Libya were briefed "on the location of approximately ten Islamist militias and AQ training camps within Benghazi . . . [and that] these groups ran the spectrum from Islamist militias, such as the QRF Brigade and Ansar al-Sharia, to 'Takfirist thugs.'"[25] What actions, if any, did you take to protect the U.S. special mission in light of the emerging high-threat environment, including the proximity of terrorist training camps?

- The *New York Times* described you as one of the driving forces behind advocating a plan to arm the Syrian rebels.[26] Were you involved in efforts to arms the Mideast rebels? Were any of these efforts centered in Libya? In the U.S. special mission in Benghazi?

- Did you mislead lawmakers when you claimed during your Benghazi testimony that you did not know whether the U.S. mission in Libya was involved in procuring or transferring weapons to Turkey and other Arab countries?

- The Senate's extensive report by its Benghazi investigative committee charged a "strong case can be made that State engaged in retaliation against witnesses who were willing to speak with Congress."[27] Were senior State officials engaged in retaliation or otherwise involved with intimidating witnesses? Did senior State officials interfere with legislative investigations into the Benghazi attacks?

TALKING POINTS PROBE

- Did the Obama administration deliberately mislead the public when it claimed the attacks were a spontaneous protest in response to a "hateful video"?

- Why were the talking points edited to remove references to *terrorism* and *al-Qaeda* in the attacks?

- Was the Obama administration in immediate possession of surveillance video from the mission that showed there was no popular protest on September 11, 2012?

- Logic dictates that spontaneous protesters do not show up with weapons, erect armed checkpoints surrounding a compound, and evidence insider knowledge of a facility while deploying military-style tactics to storm a U.S. mission. Nor do spontaneous protesters know the exact location of a secretive CIA annex, including the specific coordinates of the building that were likely utilized to launch precision mortar strikes. Spontaneous protesters are not capable of mounting a fierce, hours-long gun battle with U.S. forces stationed inside the annex. Yet the initial reports from the Obama administration blamed the attack on spontaneous protestors. How does the administration explain its rejection of logic in explaining what happened that fated night?

- What was the exact role in the talking points scandal of Mike Morell, then acting CIA director?

Morell claimed the talking points were changed to protect a criminal investigation. Did he know this was not the case?

- In June 2013, Morell announced he was stepping down from his CIA position to spend more time with his family. Did Morell, a favorite CIA chief, really leave the agency because of the talking points scandal?

- Morell later reemerged as a counselor to Beacon Global Strategies, a consultant group particularly close to Hillary Clinton.[28] Was Morell given this job in exchange for his silence in the talking points scandal?

- In February 2014 a bipartisan Senate Intelligence Committee report revealed that Morell was in receipt of critical information on September 15, 2012, one day before Rice used the talking points publicly. The report said that Morell and others at the CIA received an e-mail from the CIA's Libya station chief stating the attacks were "not an escalation of protests."[29] What did Morell do with this information?

- In perhaps one of the most damning sections of the Republican House Interim Progress Report on the events in Benghazi, lawmakers who penned the investigation wrote that they were given access to classified e-mails and other communications that prove the talking points were not edited to protect classified information but instead to protect the State Department's reputation. Who at the State

Department made the decision to alter the talking points?

- The Obama administration spent seventy thousand dollars in taxpayer funds on an ad campaign denouncing the anti-Muhammad film. The ads, featuring Clinton and President Obama, reportedly aired on seven Pakistani networks. Did the White House know at the time that anger over the film was not the motivating factor for the Benghazi attacks?

APPENDIX C

RESPONSE TO *HARD CHOICES* BY HILLARY CLINTON

Just as this book was being sent to press, Hillary Clinton released her own book, entitled *Hard Choices* (New York: Simon & Schuster, 2014), containing an extensive chapter on the Benghazi attacks. A review of the chapter finds her narrative contains misleading statements about the deadly assaults and the then secretary of state's personal role in the decision-making process.

Here are twelve significant problems with the Benghazi section of Clinton's book.

1) CLINTON CLAIMS NO RESPONSIBLE FOR BENGHAZI SECURITY.

Denying a personal role in the decision-making process regarding security of the compound, Clinton writes that she did not see the cables requesting additional security.

She claims cables related to the security at the compound were only addressed to her as a "procedural quirk" and didn't actually land on her desk.

Clinton writes: "That's not how it works. It shouldn't. And it didn't."[1]

However, as documented in chapter 7 of this book, the Senate's January 2014 report on the Benghazi attack reveals lawmakers found that the Benghazi facility required special waivers to be legally occupied, since it did not meet the minimum official security standards set by the State Department. Some of the waivers could only have been signed by Clinton herself.

Clinton would have a lot of explaining to do if she signed waivers allowing the facility to be legally occupied without reviewing the U.S. special mission's security posture.

Further, as noted in this book, the Senate found it was Clinton's top deputies, including officials known to be close to the Clintons, who were responsible for some major denials of security at the compound.

For some lawmakers, it defies logic that Clinton was not informed, especially since she was known to have taken a particular interest in the Benghazi facility. She reportedly called for the compound to be converted into a permanent mission before a scheduled trip to Libya in December 2012 that eventually was canceled.

2) CLINTON MISREPRESENTS STEVENS' REASON FOR VISITING BENGHAZI.

Clinton suggests that Ambassador Christopher Stevens

traveled to Benghazi before the attacks and implies he took meetings at the U.S. special mission that ill-fated night on his own initiative.

Clinton writes: "U.S. Ambassadors are not required to consult or seek approval from Washington when traveling within their countries, and rarely do. Like all Chiefs of Mission, Chris made decisions about his movements based on the security assessments of his team on the ground, as well as his own judgment. After all, no one had more knowledge or experience in Libya than he did."[2]

She writes that Stevens "understood Benghazi's strategic importance in Libya and decided that the value of a visit outweighed the risks." She does not provide the actual reason for Stevens' visit to the Benghazi compound.[3]

Clinton failed to mention Stevens may have gone to Benghazi for a project that she specifically requested.

Recall in chapter 7 I cited congressional testimony by Gregory Hicks, the former State Department deputy chief of mission and chargé d'affaires who was in Libya at the time of the attack, Stevens went to the compound that day in part because Clinton wanted to convert the shanty complex into a permanent mission in a symbol of the new Libya.

Hicks said Clinton wanted to announce the establishment of a permanent U.S. State Department facility during her planned visit there in December 2012. Apparently Stevens was up against a very specific funding deadline to complete an extensive survey of the mission so the compound could be converted.

He further testified that in May 2012, during a meeting with Clinton, Stevens promised he would give priority to making sure the U.S. facility at Benghazi was transformed into a permanent constituent post. Hicks said Stevens himself wanted to make a symbolic gesture to the people of Benghazi that the United States "stood behind their dream of establishing a new democracy."

3) CLINTON WHITEWASHES HER OWN BENGHAZI STATEMENT.

At about 10 p.m. Eastern on September 11, 2012, Clinton was one of the first Obama administration officials to make a public statement about the Benghazi attacks.

In her book, Clinton writes: "As the cameras snapped away, I laid out the facts as we knew them—'heavily armed militants' had assaulted our compound and killed our people—and assured Americans that we were doing everything possible to keep safe our personnel and citizens around the world. I also offered prayers for the families of the victims and praise for the diplomats who serve our country and our values all over the world."[4]

Clinton fails to mention that in her initial statement she also first linked the Benghazi attacks to the infamous anti-Islam film.

Her brief official statement included this: "Some have sought to justify this vicious behavior as a response to inflammatory material posted on the Internet. The United States deplores any intentional effort to denigrate the religious beliefs of others. Our commitment to religious tolerance goes back to the very beginning of our nation. But let me be clear: There is never any justification for violent acts of this kind."[5]

4) CLINTON LIED ABOUT THE LOCATION OF NEAREST SPECIAL FORCES.

Clinton wrongly writes that the closest U.S. special forces that could have responded to the attacks were "standing by in Fort Bragg, North Carolina, but they would take several hours to muster and were more than five thousand miles away."[6]

She continued: "Critics have questioned why the world's greatest military force could not get to Benghazi in time to defend our people. Part of the answer is that, despite having established United States Africa Command in 2008, there just wasn't much U.S. military infrastructure in place in Africa."[7]

It has been confirmed, as I extensively documented in chapter 3, that Special Forces known as C-110, or the EUCOM CIF, were on a training mission in Croatia the night of the attacks. The distance between Croatia's capital, Zagreb, and Benghazi is about 925 miles. The C-110 is a rapid-response team that exists for emergencies like terrorist attacks against U.S. embassies abroad.

Instead of being deployed to Libya, the C-110 was told the night of the attacks to return to its normal operating base in Germany.

5) CLINTON CLAIMED BEST INTELLIGENCE SUGGESTED A VIDEO SPARKED THE ATTACK.

Clinton defended the actions of then United Nations

ambassador Susan Rice, who on Sunday, September 16, 2012, infamously appeared on five morning television programs to offer the official Obama administration response to the Benghazi attack. In nearly identical statements, Rice asserted that the attack was a spontaneous protest in response to a "hateful video."

Writes Clinton: "Susan stated what the intelligence community believed, rightly or wrongly, at the time. That was the best she or anyone could do. Every step of the way, whenever something new was learned, it was quickly shared with Congress and the American people. There is a difference between getting something wrong, and committing wrong. A big difference that some have blurred to the point of casting those who made a mistake as intentionally deceitful."[8]

Clinton's claim that the intelligence community believed the attacks were a spontaneous protest in response to a "hateful video" is called into question by numerous revelations.

Stevens' deputy Hicks testified he knew immediately it was a terrorist attack, not a protest turned violent. According to Hicks, "everybody in the mission" believed it was an act of terror "from the get-go."[9]

The CIA's station chief in Libya reportedly e-mailed his superiors on the day of the attack that it was "not an escalation of anti-American protest."[10]

The claim of a popular protest also defies logic, as I noted repeatedly in this book. Spontaneous protesters do not show up with weapons, erect armed checkpoints surrounding a compound, and demonstrate insider knowledge of a facility while deploying military-style tactics to storm a U.S. mission. Nor do spontaneous protesters know the exact location of a secretive CIA annex, including the specific coordinates of a building likely utilized to launch precision mortar strikes. Spontaneous protesters are not thought to be capable of mounting a fierce, hours-long gun battle with U.S. forces stationed inside the annex.

Interestingly, Clinton's own description of the attacks does not contain any account of popular protests. She writes the attack began when, "without warning, dozens of armed men appeared at the gates of the compound, overwhelmed the local Libyan guards, and streamed inside. They set fires as they went."[11]

6) CLINTON DENIES ORDERING LOCAL CIA AGENTS TO DELAY STORMING THE COMPOUND.

Clinton does not mention any delay in the response by the CIA officers stationed about one mile from the Benghazi mission at a nearby secretive CIA annex.

She relates: "From the moment the CIA station learned their fellow Americans were under attack, a response team prepared to launch a rescue. They could hear explosions in the distance and quickly assembled their weapons and prepared to deploy. Two vehicles of armed officers left the CIA post for the diplomatic compound about twenty minutes after the attack had begun. . . . When the CIA team arrived, they split up to secure the compound and joined the DS agents in the search of the burning building."[12]

Clinton leaves out the fact that CIA agents who were on the ground in Benghazi testified to lawmakers they were loaded into vehicles and ready to aid the besieged U.S. special mission on September 11, 2012, but were told by superiors to "wait," according to reports.

Rep. Lynn Westmoreland (R-GA), head of the House intelligence subcommittee that interviewed the CIA employees, explained that while there was no "stand-down order," there was a disagreement at the nearby CIA annex about how quickly to respond. Westmoreland revealed that some CIA agents wanted to storm the Benghazi compound immediately, but they were told to wait while the agency collected intelligence on the ongoing attack.[13]

7) CLINTON CONTINUES TO PROMOTE A QUESTIONABLE "LULL IN THE FIGHTING" NARRATIVE.

In recounting the attacks, Clinton promotes the Obama administration narrative of a lull in the fighting.

She writes: "The drone was redirected to Benghazi and arrived on station roughly ninety minutes after the attack began, providing U.S. security and intelligence officials another way to monitor what was happening on the ground. Around that time the Operations Center reported that gunfire at the compound had subsided and our security forces were attempting to locate missing personnel. That was a chilling phrase. Much of the mob had withdrawn, but for how long?"[14]

However, witnesses on the ground, including CIA contractors who were inside the annex, said there was no lull in the fighting at all, as first reported by the *Daily Beast*.[15]

The lull claim was central to the Obama administration's explanation for why no air support or special forces were deployed to Benghazi, with the White House and State officials saying they believed the attack had finished and were taken by surprise when it continued.

8) CLINTON CLAIMS SHE DID NOT IGNORE SECURITY REQUESTS. Regarding security at the Benghazi mission, Clinton writes:

> Though security upgrades had been made to the Benghazi compound—including extending the height of the outer wall with masonry concrete and barbed wire; installing external lighting, concrete vehicle barriers, guard booths, and sandbag emplacements; hardening wooden doors with steel and reinforced locks; and adding equipment to detect explosives—the review board determined that these precautions were simply inadequate in an increasingly dangerous city.[16]

Clinton failed to mention her deputies were responsible for some of the most shocking security decisions made regarding the Benghazi compound.

As documented in chapter 7 of this book, it was State Department undersecretary Patrick Kennedy who canceled the use in Tripoli of a DC-3 aircraft that could have aided in the evacuation of the Benghazi victims. Kennedy also nonsensically denied guard towers to the Benghazi mission and approved the withdrawal of Security Support Teams, or

SST, special U.S. forces specifically maintained for counterattacks on U.S. embassies or threats against diplomatic personnel. The Senate's January 2014 Benghazi report found Kennedy's withdrawal of the SST was made "despite compelling requests from personnel in Libya that the team be allowed to stay."[17]

9) CLINTON BLAMES TALKING POINTS ON THE CIA.

Clinton placed the blame for the controversial talking points squarely with the CIA without mentioning the State Department contributed to the manufacturing of the points.

"The extensive public record now makes clear that Susan (Rice) was using information that originated with and was approved by the CIA," she writes. "That assessment didn't come from political operatives in the White House; it came from career professionals in the intelligence community."[18]

The Senate's January 2014 report reveals that State Department spokeswoman Victoria Nuland played an active role in crafting the talking point,s as did Clinton's deputy chief of staff, Jake Sullivan.[19]

10) CLINTON FALSELY CLAIMS SHE IMPLEMENTED ALL ACCOUNTABILITY REVIEW BOARD (ARB) RECOMMENDATIONS.

In her book, Clinton writes matter-of-factly: "The review board made twenty-nine specific recommendations (twenty-four unclassified) to address the deficiencies it found in areas such as training, fire safety, staffing, and threat analysis."[20]

She relates: "I agreed with all twenty-nine and immediately accepted them. I pledged that I would not leave office until every recommendation was on its way to implementation. By the time I left, we had met that goal."[21]

The ARB, known for minimizing Clinton's complicity in the attacks, singled out four unnamed State officials guilty of "systemic failures and leadership and management deficiencies" that contributed to the "grossly inadequate" security situation in Benghazi.[22]

Unabashed House Republicans, writing in a House Majority report, had no problem naming the four officials, all of whom served directly under Clinton.

The four officials were revealed to be Assistant Secretary for Diplomatic Security Eric Boswell, Principal Deputy Assistant Secretary of Diplomatic Security Scott Bultrowicz, Deputy Assistant Secretary of Diplomatic Security for International Programs Charlene Lamb and Deputy Assistant Secretary for Maghreb Affairs Raymond Maxwell.[23]

Despite State proclamations that those responsible would be disciplined or removed, three of the officials were reassigned to new posts. Maxwell voluntarily retired, which he had planned to do in 2012 before being delayed by the turmoil of the so-called Arab Spring. Maxwell was later found to not have contributed to security decisions in Benghazi, while the other three officials were reportedly involved in the ultimately disastrous decisions.

The House singled out Charlene Lamb, who worked closely with Clinton, for her "unwillingness to provide additional security personnel" to the Benghazi facility.

11) CLINTON BLAMES THE CAIRO PROTESTS.

Clinton seeks to connect the Benghazi jihadist assaults to popular civilian protests that took place the same day outside the U.S. embassy in Cairo. She claimed the Cairo protests were about the anti-Islam film, which led to the belief the Benghazi assaults were also about the film.

"Half a world away in Cairo, young men began gathering in the street outside the U.S. Embassy as part of a protest organized by hard-line Islamist leaders against the insulting video," she writes.[24]

However, as documented in several chapters in this book, the Cairo protests were announced days in advance as part of a movement to free the so-called blind sheikh, Omar Abdel-Rahman, who is serving a life sentence in the United States for conspiracy in the 1993 World Trade Center bombing.

Rahman's son, Abdallah Abdel Rahman, even went so far as to threaten to storm the U.S. embassy in Cairo and detain the employees inside.

In fact, on the day of the September 11, 2012, protests in Cairo, CNN's Nic Robertson interviewed Rahman's son, who described the protest as being about freeing his father. No Muhammad film was mentioned. A big banner calling for Rahman's release can be seen as Robertson walked to the embassy protests. No such banners were seen in protest of the Muhammad film.

12) CLINTON RELIED ON A QUESTIONABLE *NEW YORK TIMES* PIECE. Clinton writes that the *New York Times* later proved in an investigation that the Muhammad video was "indeed a factor" in what happened in Benghazi.

"There were scores of attackers that night, almost certainly with differing motives," she writes. "It is inaccurate to state that every single one of them was influenced by this hateful video. It is equally inaccurate to state that none of them were. Both assertions defy not only the evidence but logic as well."[25]

Clinton was referring to a December 28, 2013, *New York Times* piece by David D. Kirkpatrick titled "A Deadly Mix in Benghazi."

See chapter 9 of this book, where I extensively question the veracity of Kirkpatrick's piece, showing that various details in his article were negated by the U.S. government, Benghazi victims, and numerous previous news reports. Kirkpatrick's piece is even contradicted by his own previous reporting, as I found.

NOTES

INTRODUCTION

1. Amie Parnes, "Obama: Extremists used film 'as an excuse' to harm US interests," The Hill, September 20, 2012, http://thehill.com/homenews/administration/250813-obama-extremists-used-film-as-an-excuse-to-harm-us-interests.
2. "Transcript: Whistle-blower's account of Sept. 11 Libya terror attack," Fox News, May 8, 2013, http://www.foxnews.com/politics/2013/05/08/transcript-whistle-blower-account-sept-11-libya-terror-attack/.
3. Catherine Herridge, "Report sheds light on ex-CIA deputy director's role in Benghazi talking points," Fox News, February 4, 2014, http://www.foxnews.com/politics/2014/02/04/report-sheds-light-on-ex-cia-director-role-in-benghazi-talking-points/.
4. US Department of State, "Unclassified" ARB Report, 22–27, accessed February 26, 2014, http://www.state.gov/documents/organization/202446.pdf.
5. Eli Lake, "CIA Contractor Testimony Could Undermine Obama on Benghazi," The Daily Beast November 6, 2013 http://www.thedailybeast.com/articles/2013/11/06/cia-contractor-testimony-could-undermine-obama-on-benghazi.html.
6. Aaron Klein, "Who's lying? Benghazi witnesses vs. State Dept." WND, November 28, 2013, http://www.wnd.com/2013/11/whos-lying-benghazi-witnesses-vs-state-dept.

1. THE *REAL* "SECURITY" SITUATION AT U.S. SPECIAL MISSION

1. "U.S. Embassy Officially Opens Consular Section in Tripoli," *Tripoli Post*, August 28, 2012, http://www.tripolipost.com/articledetail.asp?c=1&i=9095.
2. U.S. Department of State, "Unclassified" ARB Report, accessed February 26, 2014, http://www.state.gov/documents/organization/202446.pdf, hereinafter "ARB report."

3. U.S. Senate Select Committee on Intelligence, *Review of the Terrorist Attacks on U.S. Facilities in Benghazi, Libya, with Additional Views*, September 11–12, 2012 (January 15, 2014), http://www.intelligence.senate.gov/benghazi2014/benghazi.pdf, 27–28.
4. Ibid., "Additional Views of Vice Chairman Chambliss and Senators Burr, Risch, Coats, Rubio, and Coburn," 12.
5. Jennifer Griffin, "EXCLUSIVE: CIA operators were denied request for help during Benghazi attack, sources say," FoxNews.com, October 26, 2012 http://www.foxnews.com/politics/2012/10/26/cia-operators-were-denied-request-for-help-during-benghazi-attack-sources-say/.
6. U.S. Senate Select Committee on Intelligence, *Review of the Terrorist Attacks on U.S. Facilities in Benghazi*, 38.
7. Ibid., 38, 39.
8. United States House of Representatives Committee on Oversight and Government Reform, "Benghazi Attacks: Investigative Update: Interim Report on the Accountability Review Board" (September 16, 2013), http://oversight.house.gov/wp-content/uploads/2013/09/Report-for-Members-final.pdf, 68.
9. Ibid., 69.
10. Ibid., 68.
11. U.S. Senate Select Committee on Intelligence, *Review of the Terrorist Attacks on U.S. Facilities in Benghazi, Additional Views*, 11.
12. Full text, Majority Staff Report, House Foreign Affairs Committee, "Benghazi: Where is the State Department Accountability?" Available at http://foreignaffairs.house.gov/sites/republicans.foreignaffairs.house.gov/files/HFAC%20Majority%20Staff%20Report%20on%20Benghazi.pdf.
13. Leigh Ann Caldwell, "GOP Rep: Benghazi Not a 'Complete Cover-Up,'" *New Day* (CNN blog), November 18, 2013, http://newday.blogs.cnn.com/2013/11/18/rep-westmoreland-weighs-in-on-hearing-with-benghazi-eye-witnesses/.
14. Vienna Convention on Diplomatic Relations of 1961, http://untreaty.un.org/ilc/texts/instruments/english/conventions/9_1_1961.pdf.
15. ARB report, 30.
16. Vienna Convention on Diplomatic Relations of 1961.
17. ARB report, 18.
18. Ibid., 5.
19. Ibid., 19.
20. Bill Roggio, "Ansar al Shariah issues statement on US Consulate assault in Libya," *Threat Matrix* (a blog of Long War Journal), September 12, 2012, http://www.longwarjournal.org/threat-matrix/archives/2012/09/ansar_al_shariah_issues_statem.php#ixzz2sT3f59rP.
21. David D. Kirkpatrick, Suliman Ali Zway, and Kareem Fahim, "Attack by Fringe Group Highlights the Problem of Libya's Militias," New York Times, Middle East, September 15, 2012, http://www.nytimes.com/2012/09/16/world/middleeast/attack-by-fringe-group-highlights-the-problem-of-libya-militias.html?pagewanted=all&_r=0.
22. "US files charges against Benghazi attack suspects, official says," FoxNews.com, August 6, 2013, http://www.foxnews.com/politics/2013/08/06/us-reportedly-files-charges-against-benghazi-attack-suspects/.
23. U.S. Senate Select Committee on Intelligence, *Review of the Terrorist Attacks on U.S. Facilities in Benghazi*, 39.
24. Ibid., 6.

25. Ibid.
26. ARB report, 21, 24.
27. Ibid., 21.
28. House Foreign Affairs Committee, "Benghazi: Where Is the State Department Accountability?" Majority Staff Report, accessed February 26, 2014, http://foreignaffairs.house.gov/sites/republicans.foreignaffairs.house.gov/files/HFAC%20Majority%20Staff%20Report%20on%20Benghazi.pdf, 12.
29. David Cenciotti, "This Is the DC-3 Plane the State Dept Denied to Stevens and Security Support Team at U.S. Embassy in Libya," *The Aviationist*, October 5, 2012, http://theaviationist.com/2012/10/05/dos-dc3/.
30. House Foreign Affairs Committee, "Benghazi," 12.
31. ARB report, 27, 28.
32. Jamie Crawford and Jill Dougherty, "State Dept. denied plane request for security team in Libya," *Security Clearance* (CNN blog), October 5, 2012, http://security.blogs.cnn.com/2012/10/05/state-dept-denied-plane-request-for-security-team-in-libya/.
33. House Foreign Affairs Committee, "Benghazi," 12.
34. Ibid.
35. Caldwell, "GOP Rep: Benghazi Not a 'Complete Cover-Up'" (Video), http://newday.blogs.cnn.com/2013/11/18/rep-westmoreland-weighs-in-on-hearing-with-benghazi-eye-witnesses/.
36. "VIDEO: Rep. Lynn Westmoreland on Benghazi eyewitness testimony," Fox News, November 26, 2013, http://video.foxnews.com/v/2871289782001/rep-lynn-westmoreland-on-benghazi-eyewitness-testimony/#sp=show-clips.
37. ARB report, 20, 21.
38. Ibid., 21.
39. Ibid., 21, 22.
40. U.S. Senate Select Committee on Intelligence, *Review of the Terrorist Attacks on U.S. Facilities in Benghazi, Additional Views*, 11.
41. Ibid.
42. Ibid., 1.
43. U.S. Senate Select Committee on Intelligence, *Review of the Terrorist Attacks on U.S. Facilities in Benghazi*, 1n2.
44. Jake Tapper, "Exclusive: Dozens of CIA operatives on the ground during Benghazi attack," *The Lead* (CNN blog), August 1, 2013, http://thelead.blogs.cnn.com/2013/08/01/exclusive-dozens-of-cia-operatives-on-the-ground-during-benghazi-attack/.

2. "FAST AND FURIOUS" OF THE MIDDLE EAST

1. For more on this, see Aaron Klein, "Sources: Slain U.S. ambassador recruited jihadists," WND, September 24, 2012, http://www.wnd.com/2012/09/sources-slain-u-s-ambassador-recruited-jihadists/.
2. Olivier Knox, "Obama administration denies role in arming Syrian rebels," ABC News, May 17, 2012, http://abcnews.go.com/Politics/OTUS/obama-administration-denies-role-arming-syrian-rebels/story?id=16364484; and David Taylor, "US admits plan to arm Syrian rebels in aftermath of chemical weapons claim," *Times* (UK), Middle East, May 2, 2013, http://www.thetimes.co.uk/tto/news/world/middleeast/article3753481.ece.

3. Aaron Klein, "Did Hillary commit perjury?" WND, March 28, 2013, http://www.wnd.com/2013/03/did-hillary-commit-perjury/.
4. Steven Lee Myers, "For Veteran Envoy, Return to Libya Was Full of Hope," *New York Times*, September 12, 2012, http://www.nytimes.com/2012/09/13/world/middleeast/for-veteran-envoy-return-to-libya-was-full-of-hope.html?_r=1&.
5. Mark Hosenball, "Exclusive: Obama authorizes secret help for Libya rebels," Reuters, March 30, 2011, http://www.reuters.com/article/2011/03/30/us-libya-usa-order-idUSTRE72T6H220110330.
6. Robert Fisk, "America's secret plan to arm Libya's rebels," *Independent* (UK), March 7, 2011, http://www.independent.co.uk/news/world/middle-east/americas-secret-plan-to-arm-libyas-rebels-2234227.html.
7. James Risen, Mark Mazzetti, and Michael S. Schmidt, "U.S.-Approved Arms for Libya Rebels Fell into Jihadis' Hands," *New York Times*, December 5, 2012, http://www.nytimes.com/2012/12/06/world/africa/weapons-sent-to-libyan-rebels-with-us-approval-fell-into-islamist-hands.html?pagewanted=all.
8. Praveen Swami, Nick Squires, and Duncan Gardham, "Libyan rebel commander admits his fighters have al-Qaeda links," *Telegraph* (UK), March 25, 2011, http://www.telegraph.co.uk/news/worldnews/africaandindianocean/libya/8407047/Libyan-rebel-commander-admits-his-fighters-have-al-Qaeda-links.html.
9. Robert Winnett, and Duncan Gardham, "Libya: al-Qaeda among Libya rebels, Nato chief fears," *Telegraph* (UK), March 29, 2011, http://www.telegraph.co.uk/news/worldnews/africaandindianocean/libya/8414583/Libya-al-Qaeda-among-Libya-rebels-Nato-chief-fears.html.
10. C. J. Chivers and Eric Schmitt, "Arms Airlift to Syria Rebels Expands, with Aid from C.I.A.," *New York Times*, March 24, 2013, http://www.nytimes.com/2013/03/25/world/middleeast/arms-airlift-to-syrian-rebels-expands-with-cia-aid.html?_r=0.
11. Ibid.
12. Risen, Mazzetti, and S. Schmidtt, "U.S.-Approved Arms for Libya Rebels Fell Into Jihadis' Hands," *New York Times*, December 5, 2012, http://www.nytimes.com/2012/12/06/world/africa/weapons-sent-to-libyan-rebels-with-us-approval-fell-into-islamist-hands.html?pagewanted=all.
13. Ibid.
14. Ibid.
15. See video, "Sen. Graham claims Benghazi survivors 'told to be quiet' by administration," Fox News, March 15, 2013, http://www.foxnews.com/politics/2013/03/15/sen-graham-claims-benghazi-survivors-told-to-be-quiet-by-administration/.
16. Catherine Herridge and Pamela Browne, "Was Syrian weapons shipment factor in ambassador's Benghazi visit?" Fox News, October 25, 2012, http://www.foxnews.com/politics/2012/10/25/was-syrian-weapons-shipment-factor-in-ambassadors-benghazi-visit/.
17. Jake Tapper, "Exclusive: Dozens of CIA operatives on the ground during Benghazi attack," *The Lead* (CNN blog), August 1, 2013, http://thelead.blogs.cnn.com/2013/08/01/exclusive-dozens-of-cia-operatives-on-the-ground-during-benghazi-attack/.
18. The Stimson Institute, "Spotlight: Assistant Secretary Shapiro Discusses Libya's Missing," February 2, 2012, http://www.stimson.org/spotlight/assistant-secretary-shapiro-discusses-libyas-missing-weapons/.

19. Jessica Donati, Ghaith Shennib and Firas Bosalum, "The adventures of a Libyan weapons dealer in Syria," Reuters, June 18, 2013, http://www.reuters.com/article/2013/06/18/us-libya-syria-idUSBRE95H0WC20130618.
20. Herridge and Browne, "Was Syrian weapons shipment factor in ambassador's Benghazi visit?"
21. Donati, Shennib, and Bosalum, "The adventures of a Libyan weapons dealer in Syria."
22. Ibid.
23. Jennifer Griffin and Adam Housley, "EXCLUSIVE: Petraeus mistress may have revealed classified information at Denver speech on real reason for Libya attack," Fox News.com, November 12, 2012, http://www.foxnews.com/politics/2012/11/12/petraeus-mistress-may-have-revealed-classified-information-at-denver-speech/.
24. Aaron Klein, "See video of Petraeus' mistress YouTube yanked," WND, November 12, 2012, http://www.wnd.com/2012/11/petraeus-mistress-speech-yanked-from-youtube/.
25. "LIBYA: Petraeus Mistress Reveals CIA Annex Had Prisoners & Maybe the Reason for Consulate Attack," YouTube video, 3:02, from a a keynote address at a University of Denver alumni symposium, given by Paula Broadwell, October 26, 2012, posted by "VexZeen," May 11, 2013, http://www.youtube.com/watch?v=WDRi72r4yLk.
26. Neil Munro, "CIA denies claim from Petraeus' girlfriend that Benghazi annex held Libyan prisoners," *Daily Caller*, November 12, 2012, http://dailycaller.com/2012/11/12/cia-denies-claim-from-petraeus-girlfriend-that-benghazi-annex-held-libyan-prisoners/.
27. The Issa quotations in this section are taken from the interview transcript available at "Darrell Issa on Benghazi and the IRS," HughHewitt.com, August 7, 2013, http://www.hughhewitt.com/darrell-issa-on-where-the-investigations-are-on-benghazi-and-irs-scandals/.

3. WHY NO SPECIAL FORCES OR AIR SUPPORT WERE SENT

1. Greg Richter, "Gen. Dempsey: No Stand Down Order Issued in Benghazi," *Newsmax*, June 12, 2013, http://www.newsmax.com/Newsfront/dempsey-benghazi-stand-down/2013/06/12/id/509608.
2. Adam Housley, "Special forces could've responded to Benghazi attack, whistle-blower tells Fox News," Fox News Politics, April 30, 2013, http://www.foxnews.com/politics/2013/04/30/special-ops-benghazi-whistleblower-tells-fox-news-government-could-have/.
3. Mark Thompson, "Second-Guessing Benghazi (Cont.)," *Time*, June 14, 2013, http://nation.time.com/2013/06/14/second-guessing-benghazi-cont/.
4. Housley, "Special forces could've responded to Benghazi attack."
5. "Transcript: Whistle-blower's account of Sept. 11 Libya terror attack," Fox News, May 8, 2013, http://www.foxnews.com/politics/2013/05/08/transcript-whistle-blower-account-sept-11-libya-terror-attack/.
6. Video available at Aspen Institute website, "AFRICOM: The Next Afghanistan?" retrieved February 2, 2014, http://www.aspeninstitute.org/events/2013/07/19/africa-newest-global-terrorism-center.

7. U.S. Department of State, "Unclassified" ARB Report, accessed February 26, 2014, http://www.state.gov/documents/organization/202446.pdf (hereinafter "ARB report"), 23.
8. Kimberly Dozier, "CIA Benghazi team clash led to 'stand down' report," Associated Press, December 14, 2013, http://bigstory.ap.org/article/cia-benghazi-team-clash-led-stand-down-report.
9. Ibid.
10. Ibid.
11. ARB report, 23.
12. Jake Tapper, "President Obama Begs Off Answering Whether Americans in Benghazi Were Denied Requests for Help," *Political Punch* (ABC blog), October 26, 2012, http://abcnews.go.com/blogs/politics/2012/10/president-obama-begs-off-answering-whether-americans-in-benghazi-were-denied-requests-for-help/.
13. ARB report, 27.
14. Cathy Burke, "Report: 400 US Surface-to-Air Missiles Went Missing in Benghazi," *Newsmax*, August 12, 2013, http://www.newsmax.com/Newsfront/surface-air-missing-missiles/2013/08/12/id/520026.
15. Ibid.
16. Awr Hawkins, "Attorney for Whistleblower: 400 U.S. Missiles Stolen in Benghazi," *Breitbart*, August 12, 2013, http://www.breitbart.com/Big-Peace/2013/08/12/Attorney-For-Benghazi-Whistleblower-400-U-S-Missiles-Stolen-In-Benghazi-Annex-Involved.
17. Burke, "Report."
18. ARB report, 27.
19. "AFRICOM and SOCAFRICA and the Terrorist Attacks in Benghazi, Libya on September 11, 2012" (transcript of unclassified witness testimony to the House Armed Services Committee), June 26, 2013, http://armedservices.house.gov/index.cfm/files/serve?File_id=AAEBCAA5-4C8F-4820-BACD-2DB9B53C3424, 46.
20. Transcript of unclassified witness testimony to the House Armed Services Committee, May 21, 2013, http://armedservices.house.gov/index.cfm/files/serve?File_id=A5BE5DFD-FAA6-4485-9D40-BA30B550907C, 47.
21. Aaron Klein, "Did senator drop Benghazi bombshell?" WND, March 18, 2013, http://www.wnd.com/2013/03/did-senator-drop-benghazi-bombshell/.
22. The Stimson Institute, "Spotlight. Assistant Secretary Shapiro Discusses Libya's Missing," February 2, 2012, http://www.stimson.org/spotlight/assistant-secretary-shapiro-discusses-libyas-missing-weapons/; "A/S SHAPIRO: STIMSON REMARKS: Addressing the Challenge of MANPADS Proliferation 2/2/12," http://www.stimson.org/images/uploads/Shapiro_Libya_Remarks.pdf, p. 1. The Shapiro comments that follow are from this transcript.
23. A/S SHAPIRO: STIMSON REMARKS, 7, 8, 9.
24. Ibid., 9, 10.
25. Ibid., 10.
26. Ibid., 12–13.
27. Ibid., 10.
28. Ibid., 15.
29. Ibid., 17.
30. Michelle Nichols, "Libya arms fueling conflicts in Syria, Mali and beyond: U.N. experts," Reuters, April 9, 2013, http://www.reuters.com/article/2013/04/09/us-libya-arms-un-idUSBRE93814Y20130409.

31. Sharyl Attkisson, "Thousands of Libyan missiles from Qaddafi era missing in action," CBS News, March 25, 2013, http://www.cbsnews.com/news/thousands-of-libyan-missiles-from-qaddafi-era-missing-in-action/.

4. AMBASSADOR STEVENS KIDNAPPED?

1. Aaron Klein, "Benghazi investigator won't deny Stevens kidnap plot," WND, September 25, 2013, http://www.wnd.com/2013/09/benghazi-investigator-wont-deny-stevens-kidnap-plot.
2. Bill Gertz, "Possible Poisoning: Al Qaeda weapons expert says U.S. ambassador to Libya killed by lethal injection," *Washington Free Beacon*, June 5, 2013, http://freebeacon.com/possible-poisoning/.
3. Ibid.
4. Ibid.
5. Office of the Spokesperson, "Background Briefing on Libya," U.S. Department of State, October 9, 2012, http://www.state.gov/r/pa/prs/ps/2012/10/198791.htm.
6. Bradley Klapper, "Timeline of comments on attack on US Consulate," Associated Press, October 27, 2012, http://bigstory.ap.org/article/timeline-comments-attack-us-consulate.
7. "Deputy Asst. Secretary of State Charlene Lamb testimony before House Oversight Committee," October 10, 2012, http://oversight.house.gov/wp-content/uploads/2012/10/2012-10-09-Lamb-Testimony-FINAL1.pdf; and Jamie Dettmer, "The Truth behind the Benghazi Attack," *Daily Beast*, October 22, 2012, http://www.thedailybeast.com/newsweek/2012/10/21/truth-behind-the-benghazi-attack.html.
8. U.S. Department of State, "Unclassified" ARB Report, accessed February 26, 2014, http://www.state.gov/documents/organization/202446.pdf (hereinafter "ARB report"), 21.
9. Ibid., 22.
10. Catherine Herridge, "Congressman: Benghazi attackers knew location of ambassador's safe room," Fox News, November 15, 2013, http://www.foxnews.com/politics/2013/11/15/benghazi-attackers-reportedly-knew-location-ambassador-safe-room/.
11. ARB report, 22.
12. Ibid.
13. Ibid., 26.
14. Ibid.
15. Ibid.
16. Ibid., 27.
17. "Transcript: Whistle-blower's account of Sept. 11 Libya terror attack," Fox News, May 8, 2013, http://www.foxnews.com/politics/2013/05/08/transcript-whistle-blower-account-sept-11-libya-terror-attack/.
18. Eli Lake and Josh Rogin, "Exclusive: Benghazi Whistleblower Says He Was Smeared," *Daily Beast*, November 2, 2013, http://www.thedailybeast.com/articles/2013/11/02/exclusive-benghazi-whistleblower-says-he-was-smeared.html.
19. "Incident Report-new1.pdf," the text of the Blue Mountain incident report at the U.S. special mission, dated September 14, 2012, can be viewed and downloaded at http://www.scribd.com/doc/181057020/Incident-Report-new1-pdf.

20. Associated Press, "US ambassador Chris Stevens killed in consulate attack in Libya," *Syracuse Post-Standard*, September 12, 2012, http://www.syracuse.com/news/index.ssf/2012/09/us_ambassador_chris_stevens_ki.html.
21. Kerry Picket, "AFP not behind report of purported rape of murdered U.S. ambassador to Libya," *Washington Times*, September 13, 2012, http://www.washingtontimes.com/blog/watercooler/2012/sep/13/picket-report-murdered-us-ambassador-libya-reporte/.
22. U.S. Senate Select Committee on Intelligence, *Review of the Terrorist Attacks on U.S. Facilities in Benghazi, Libya, with Additional Views*, September 11–12, 2012 January 15, 2014, http://www.intelligence.senate.gov/benghazi2014/benghazi.pdf, 6.
23. Ibid., 7–8.

5. WHODUNIT?

1. Bill Roggio, "Ansar al Shariah issues statement on US Consulate assault in Libya," *Threat Matrix* (a blog of the Long War Journal), September 12, 2012, http://www.longwarjournal.org/threat-matrix/archives/2012/09/ansar_al_shariah_issues_statem.php#ixzz2sT3f59rP.
2. David D. Kirkpatrick, Suliman Ali Zway, and Kareem Fahim, "Attack by Fringe Group Highlights the Problem of Libya's Militias," *New York Times*, Middle East, September 15, 2012, http://www.nytimes.com/2012/09/16/world/middleeast/attack-by-fringe-group-highlights-the-problem-of-libya-militias.html?pagewanted=all&_r=0.
3. David D. Kirkpatrick , "Suspect in Libya Attack, in Plain Sight, Scoffs at U.S." *New York Times*, Africa, October 18, 2012, http://www.nytimes.com/2012/10/19/world/africa/suspect-in-benghazi-attack-scoffs-at-us.html?pagewanted=all&_r=1&.
4. Adam Goldman, "Former Guantanamo detainee implicated in Benghazi attack," *Washington Post*, January 8, 2014, http://www.washingtonpost.com/world/national-security/former-guantanamo-detainee-implicated-in-benghazi-attack/2014/01/07/c73fdf78-77d5-11e3-8963-b4b654bcc9b2_story.html.
5. Federal Research Division, Library of Congress, "Al-Qaida in Libya: A Profile" (Washington, D.C., August 2012), http://www.fas.org/irp/world/para/aq-libya-loc.pdf, 17.
6. Ibid., 3, 6, 23.
7. Ibid., 1.
8. Ibid., 12.
9. Aaron Klein, "Egypt's Morsi behind murder of U.S. ambassador?" WND, July 7, 2013, http://www.wnd.com/2013/07/egypts-morsi-behind-murder-of-u-s-ambassador. See also Raymond Ibrahim, "Libyan Intelligence: Morsi, Muslim Brotherhood Involved in Benghazi, *Front Page* magazine, June 27, 2013, posted at http://www.freerepublic.com/focus/news/3036218/posts.
10. Josh Rogin, "Exclusive: John McCain on His Meeting with the Muslim Brotherhood in Cairo," *Daily Beast*, August 6, 2013, http://www.thedailybeast.com/articles/2013/08/06/exclusive-john-mccain-on-his-meeting-with-the-muslim-brotherhood-in-cairo.html.

11. See, for example, "Video storm the U.S. embassy and burned in Libya," Arabic-language YouTube video, 2:19, purporting to show Benghazi attackers speaking Egyptian dialect, posted by "Morad709," September 12, 2012, http://www.youtube.com/watch?v=wSXHsTCFysI.
12. Cynthia Farahat, "Benghazi Terrorists: 'Dr. Morsi Sent Us,'" *Front Page* magazine, May 31, 2013, http://www.frontpagemag.com/2013/cynthia-farahat/benghazi-terrorists-dr-morsi-sent-us/.
13. Klein, "Egypt's Morsi behind murder of U.S. ambassador?"
14. Warner Todd Huston, "CNN Ignores Real Goal of Cairo Riots: Freedom of Blind Sheik," *Breitbart News*, September 14, 2012, http://www.breitbart.com/Big-Journalism/2012/09/13/Cairo-Riots-Were-Not-Over-Offensive-American-Movie-Freedom-of-Blind-Sheik-The-Goal.
15. US Department of State, "Unclassified" ARB Report, accessed February 26, 2014, http://www.state.gov/documents/organization/202446.pdf, 16.
16. "EDITORIAL: Obama's intelligence failure," *Washington Times*, September 16, 2012, http://www.washingtontimes.com/news/2012/sep/16/obamas-intelligence-failure/.
17. Nic Robertson, Paul Cruickshank, and Tim Lister, "Pro-al Qaeda group seen behind deadly Benghazi attack," CNN, September 13, 2012, http://edition.cnn.com/2012/09/12/world/africa/libya-attack-jihadists.
18. Josh Gerstein, "Ex-FBI agent admits to AP leak," *Politico*, September 23, 2013, http://www.politico.com/story/2013/09/ex-fbi-agent-pleads-guilty-associated-press-leak-case-97226.html.
19. U.S. Department of State Office of the Spokesperson, "Terrorist Designations of the Muhammad Jamal Network and Muhammad Jamal," State.gov, October 7, 2013, http://www.state.gov/r/pa/prs/ps/2013/10/215171.htm.
20. U.S. Senate Select Committee on Intelligence, *Review of the Terrorist Attacks on U.S. Facilities in Benghazi, Libya, with Additional Views*, September 11–12, 2012 January 15, 2014, http://www.intelligence.senate.gov/benghazi2014/benghazi.pdf, 40.
21. United Nations, Security Council Committee pursuant to resolutions 1267 (1999) and 1989 (2011) concerning Al-Qaida and associated individuals and entities, "Narrative Summaries of Reasons for Listing," United Nations website, accessed February 12, 2014, http://www.un.org/sc/committees/1267/NSQE13613E.shtml.
22. Eli Lake, "Benghazi's Al Qaeda Connection," *Daily Beast*, October 7, 2013, http://www.thedailybeast.com/articles/2013/10/07/benghazi-s-al-qaeda-connection.html.
23. Aaron Klein, "Look who freed Benghazi attackers," WND, October 8, 2013, http://www.wnd.com/2013/10/look-who-freed-benghazi-attackers.
24. "Al-Qaeda confirms death of bin Laden confidant Libi," *Daily Star* (Lebanon), September 11, 2012, http://www.dailystar.com.lb/News/Middle-East/2012/Sep-11/187485-al-qaeda-confirms-death-of-bin-laden-confidant-libi.ashx#axzz2t2qejB4l.
25. Paul Cruickshank et al., "Sources: 3 al Qaeda operatives took part in Benghazi attack," CNN, May 4, 2013, http://edition.cnn.com/2013/05/02/world/africa/us-libya-benghazi-suspects/index.html.
26. Kirkpatrick , "Suspect in Libya Attack, in Plain Sight, Scoffs at U.S."
27. July Pace, "Vanishing adviser reappears as Iran policy player," Associated Press, December 24, 2013, http://news.yahoo.com/vanishing-adviser-reappears-iran-policy-player-185811990--politics.html.

28. Guy Taylor, "Benghazi talking points not shared with Clinton, Nuland says," *Washington Times*, July 11, 2013, http://www.washingtontimes.com/news/2013/jul/11/clinton-aide-victoria-nuland-promotion-faces-senat/?page=all.
29. Larry Johnson, "Was Iran behind Benghazi?" *No Quarter* (blog), October 25, 2012, http://www.noquarterusa.net/blog/73784/was-iran-behind-benghazi/.
30. Mark Langfan, "Op-Ed: Benghazi Leads to Iran, Not Al Qaeda," Arutz Sheva 7 / Israel National News, August 3, 2013, http://www.israelnationalnews.com/Articles/Article.aspx/13641#.Ut6iTRD8LX5.
31. Marinka Peschmann, "Whistleblower Exclusive: The Benghazi cover-up is the proxy battle with the war with Iran," *Canada Free Press*, May 29, 2013, http://www.canadafreepress.com/index.php/article/55502.

6. THE *REAL* REASON BENGHAZI SUSPECTS NOT CAPTURED

1. Evan Perez, "First criminal charges filed in Benghazi attack probe," CNN, August 7, 2013, http://edition.cnn.com/2013/08/06/politics/benghazi-charges/index.html.
2. David D. Kirkpatrick, "Suspect in Libya Attack, in Plain Sight, Scoffs at U.S." *New York Times*, Africa, October 18, 2012, http://www.nytimes.com/2012/10/19/world/africa/suspect-in-benghazi-attack-scoffs-at-us.html?pagewanted=all&_r=1&.
3. Bill Roggio, "Ansar al Shariah issues statement on US Consulate assault in Libya," *Threat Matrix* (a blog of Long War Journal), September 12, 2012, http://www.longwarjournal.org/threat-matrix/archives/2012/09/ansar_al_shariah_issues_statem.php#ixzz2sT3f59rP.
4. Kirkpatrick, "Suspect in Libya Attack, in Plain Sight, Scoffs at U.S."
5. "Grand Jury Indictment of Abu Anas al-Libi," *New York Times*, October 5, 2013, http://www.nytimes.com/interactive/2013/10/05/world/africa/06libya-document.html?_r=0.
6. Esam Mohamed and Robert Burns, "Anas al-Libi, Libyan Militant, Reportedly Captured In Tripoli," Associated Press article reprinted at the *World Post*, October 5, 2013, http://www.huffingtonpost.com/2013/10/05/abu-anas-al-libi-libya_n_4050844.html.
7. Barbara Starr, "First on CNN: US commandos were poised for raid to capture Benghazi suspect," *Security Clearance* (CNN blog), October 29, 2013, http://security.blogs.cnn.com/2013/10/29/first-on-cnn-us-commandos-were-poised-for-raid-to-capture-benghazi-suspect/.
8. Michael S. Schmidt and Eric Schmitt, "U.S. Officials Say Libya Approved Commando Raids," *New York Times*, October 9, 2013, http://www.nytimes.com/2013/10/09/world/africa/us-officials-say-libya-approved-commando-raids.html?adxnnl=1&adxnnlx=1389711914-LSs9DhQpRflj/2xN21X9Mg.
9. Ibid.
10. Starr, "First on CNN."
11. Ibid.
12. Schmidt and Schmitt, "U.S. Officials Say Libya Approved Commando Raids."
13. Mark Thiessen, "Kidnapped Libyan prime minister pays the price for an Obama leak," *Washington Post*, October 10, 2013, http://www.washingtonpost.com/opinions/marc-thiessen-the-consequences-of-an-obama-administration-leak/2013/10/10/cfd5b43c-31ad-11e3-8627-c5d7de0a046b_story.html.

14. Adam Goldman and Sari Horwitz, "U.S. efforts stall in capturing suspects in 2012 Benghazi attacks, officials say," *Washington Post*, December 6, 2013, http://www.washingtonpost.com/world/national-security/us-efforts-stall-in-capturing-suspects-in-2012-benghazi-attacks-officials-say/2013/12/05/4847afe4-5dd0-11e3-95c2-13623eb2b0e1_story.html.
15. Ibid.

7. GAME CHANGER: HILLARY'S CENTRAL, UNREPORTED ROLE IN BENGHAZI

1. "Hillary Clinton at Benghazi Hearing: 'What Difference, Does It Make. . . ,'" YouTube video, 1:08, posted by Joe Bunting, http://www.youtube.com/watch?v=Ka0_nz53CcM; accessed March 17, 2014.
2. U.S. Senate Select Committee on Intelligence, *Review of the Terrorist Attacks on U.S. Facilities in Benghazi, Libya, with Additional Views*, September 11–12, 2012 January 15, 2014, http://www.intelligence.senate.gov/benghazi2014/benghazi.pdf, "Additional Views of Vice Chairman Chambliss and Senators Burr, Risch, Coats, Rubio, and Coburn," 11.
3. U.S. State Department, "Benghazi: Where Is the State Department Accountability?" Majority Staff Report – House Foreign Affairs Committee, accessed March 17, 2014, http://foreignaffairs.house.gov/sites/republicans.foreignaffairs.house.gov/files/HFAC%20Majority%20Staff%20Report%20on%20Benghazi.pdf, 7.
4. Ibid., 12.
5. US Department of State, "Unclassified" ARB Report, accessed February 26, 2014, http://www.state.gov/documents/organization/202446.pdf (hereinafter "ARB report"), 30.
6. U.S. Senate Select Committee on Intelligence, *Review of the Terrorist Attacks on U.S. Facilities in Benghazi, Libya, Additional Views of Vice Chairman Chambliss and Senators Burr, Risch, Coats, Rubio, and Coburn*, 10.
7. Ibid.
8. ARB report, 4, 29.
9. U.S. State Department, "Benghazi: Where Is the State Department Accountability?" 10.
10. Brian Knowlton, "U.S. Diplomats, Relieved after Libyan Attack, Are Reinstated," *New York Times*, August 20, 2013, http://www.nytimes.com/2013/08/21/world/africa/us-diplomats-relieved-after-libyan-attack-are-reinstated.html?_r=0.
11. Maxwell admitted this during a May 7, 2013, interview with the House Foreign Affairs Committee as referenced on page 10 of the Committee's Majority Staff Report, "Benghazi: Where Is the State Department Accountability?" (See note 3.)
12. Ibid., 13.
13. U.S. Senate Select Committee on Intelligence, *Review of the Terrorist Attacks on U.S. Facilities in Benghazi, Libya, Additional Views of Vice Chairman Chambliss and Senators Burr, Risch, Coats, Rubio, and Coburn*, 9.
14. U.S. State Department, "Benghazi: Where Is the State Department Accountability?" 13.
15. Stephen F. Hayes, "Lawmakers: CIA #2 Lied to Us about Benghazi," *Weekly Standard*, March 3, 2014, http://www.weeklystandard.com/blogs/lawmakers-cia-2-lied-us-about-benghazi_782724.html.

16. "TRANSCRIPTS Hillary Clinton Senate Hearing: Questions from Senators Flake, Coons, and McCain," CNN.com, January 23, 2013, http://transcripts.cnn.com/TRANSCRIPTS/1301/23/cnr.04.html.
17. U.S. House of Representatives, "Interim Progress Report for the Members of the House Republican Conference on the Events Surrounding the September 11, 2012 Terrorist Attacks in Benghazi, Libya," April 23, 2013, https://goodlatte.house.gov/system/uploads/229/original/Libya-Progress-Report.pdf, 6.
18. U.S. Senate Select Committee on Intelligence, *Review of the Terrorist Attacks on U.S. Facilities in Benghazi, Libya, Additional Views of Vice Chairman Chambliss and Senators Burr, Risch, Coats, Rubio, and Coburn*, 11.
19. Catherine Herridge, "Exclusive: Classified cable warned consulate couldn't withstand 'coordinated attack,'" Fox News Politics, October 31, 2012, http://www.foxnews.com/politics/2012/10/31/exclusive-us-memo-warned-libya-consulate-couldnt-withstand-coordinated-attack/.
20. Terence P. Jeffrey, "Testimony: Stevens Went to Benghazi Mission on 9/11/12 So Clinton Could Announce on Upcoming Libyan Visit It Had Become Permanent U.S. Post," CNS News, May 9, 2013, http://cnsnews.com/news/article/testimony-stevens-went-benghazi-mission-91112-so-clinton-could-announce-upcoming-libyan.
21. Ibid.
22. Ibid.
23. Michael R. Gordon and Mark Landler, "Backstage Glimpses of Clinton as Dogged Diplomat, Win or Lose," *New York Times*, February 2, 2013, http://www.nytimes.com/2013/02/03/us/politics/in-behind-scene-blows-and-triumphs-sense-of-clinton-future.html?action=click&module=Search®ion=searchResults%230&version=&url=http%3A%2F%2Fquery.nytimes.com%2Fsearch%2Fsitesearch%2F%23%2FBackstage%2BGlimpses%2Bof%2BClinton%2Bas%2BDogged%2BDiplomat%2C%2BWin%2Bor%2BLose%2F.
24. C. J. Chivers and Eric Schmitt, "Arms Airlift to Syria Rebels Expands, with Aid from C.I.A.," *New York Times*, March 24, 2013, http://www.nytimes.com/2013/03/25/world/middleeast/arms-airlift-to-syrian-rebels-expands-with-cia-aid.html?_r=0.
25. Catherine Herridge, "Letter questions whether Boehner was briefed on Benghazi ops," Fox News Politics, January 8, 2014, http://www.foxnews.com/politics/2014/01/08/letter-questions-whether-boehner-was-briefed-on-benghazi-ops/.

8. THE *REAL* STORY OF THOSE PESKY TALKING POINTS

1. See "Ambassador Rice spends Sunday reinforcing White House position that Middle East violence was 'spontaneous'" Fox News Politics, September 16, 2012, http://www.foxnews.com/politics/2012/09/16/us-ambassador-rice-backs-administration-violence-sparked-by-anti-muslim-video/.
2. Amie Parnes, "Obama: Extremists used film 'as an excuse' to harm US interests," *The Hill*, September 20, 2012, http://thehill.com/homenews/administration/250813-obama-extremists-used-film-as-an-excuse-to-harm-us-interests.
3. U.S. House of Representatives, "Interim Progress Report for the Members of the House Republican Conference on the Events Surrounding the September 11, 2012 Terrorist Attacks in Benghazi, Libya," April 23, 2013, http://oversight.house.gov/wp-content/uploads/2013/04/Libya-Progress-Report-Final-1.pdf, 3. Hereinafter, House, Interim Progress Report.

4. See page 2, bullet point 2 under the heading "4:42 p.m." of the image at http://abcnews.go.com/images/Politics/Benghazi%20Talking%20Points%20Timeline.pdf.
5. Lindsey Boerma, "Official: We knew Benghazi was a terrorist attack 'from the get-go,'" CBS News, May 5, 2013, http://www.cbsnews.com/news/official-we-knew-benghazi-was-a-terrorist-attack-from-the-get-go/.
6. Robin Banerji, "Did Ansar al-Sharia carry out Libya attack?" BBC Africa, September 12, 2012, http://www.bbc.com/news/world-africa-19575753.
7. Leila Fadel, "Consulate Attack Preplanned, Libya's President Says," NPR, September 16, 2012, http://www.npr.org/2012/09/16/161228170/consulate-attack-preplanned-libya-s-president-says.
8. Tabassum Zakaria and Mark Hosenball, "Shifting account of CIA's Libya talking points fuels Rice controversy," Reuters, November 28, 2012, http://www.reuters.com/article/2012/11/29/us-usa-benghazi-rice-cia-idUSBRE8AS03F20121129.
9. "Statement from Senators Graham, McCain, and Ayotte," Press Room (Senator Graham's official press release website), November 27, 2012, http://www.lgraham.senate.gov/public/index.cfm?FuseAction=PressRoom.PressReleases&ContentRecord_id=44354784-f8c9-664b-6178-c23a24d5c1ee&IsPrint=true.
10. Sharyl Attkisson, "Who changed the Benghazi talking points?" CBS News, November 28, 2012, http://www.cbsnews.com/news/who-changed-the-benghazi-talking-points/; http://www.cbsnews.com/8301-250_162-57555984/who-changed-the-benghazi-talking-points/.
11. "Statement from Senators Graham, McCain, and Ayotte."
12. Zakaria and Hosenball, "Shifting account of CIA's Libya talking points fuels Rice controversy."
13. Attkisson, "Who changed the Benghazi talking points?"
14. Rachel Rose Hartman, "Deputy CIA Director Morell to retire to 'spend more time with family'" Yahoo! News, June 12, 2013, http://news.yahoo.com/blogs/ticket/deputy-cia-director-michael-morell-retire-replaced-white-200541735.html.
15. Stephen F. Hayes, "Lawmakers: CIA #2 Lied to Us about Benghazi," *Weekly Standard*, March 3, 2014, http://www.weeklystandard.com/blogs/lawmakers-cia-2-lied-us-about-benghazi_782724.html.
16. Philippe I. Reines bio at Beacon Global Strategies website, accessed March 17, 2014, http://beaconglobalstrategies.com/team/philippe-i-reines/.
17. Catherine Herridge, "Report sheds light on ex-CIA deputy director's role in Benghazi talking points," Fox News Politics, February 04, 2014, http://www.foxnews.com/politics/2014/02/04/report-sheds-light-on-ex-cia-director-role-in-benghazi-talking-points/.
18. House, Interim Progress Report, 3.
19. Ibid., 19, 3; emphasis added.
20. Ibid., 3.
21. Ibid., 20; emphasis added.
22. Associated Press, "State Department spending $70G on Pakistan ads denouncing anti-Islam film," Fox News Politics, September 20, 2012, http://www.foxnews.com/politics/2012/09/20/state-department-spending-70g-on-pakistan-ads-denouncing-anti-islam-film/.
23. "'Innocence of Muslims' filmmaker arrested on probation violation," *L.A. Now* (*Los Angeles Times* blog), September 27, 2012, http://latimesblogs.latimes.com/lanow/2012/09/innocence-of-muslims-filmmaker-arrested-on-probation-violation.html.

24. The Hicks quotations that follow are from "Transcript: Whistle-blower's account of Sept. 11 Libya terror attack," Fox News, May 8, 2013, http://www.foxnews.com/politics/2013/05/08/transcript-whistle-blower-account-sept-11-libya-terror-attack/.
25. US Department of State, "Unclassified" ARB Report, accessed February 26, 2014, http://www.state.gov/documents/organization/202446.pdf, 25.
26. Ibid., 25, 27.

9. NEWS MEDIA SNAGGED IN BENGHAZI DECEPTION

1. David D. Kirkpatrick, "A Deadly Mix in Benghazi," chap. 1, *New York Times*, December 28, 2013, http://www.nytimes.com/projects/2013/benghazi/#/?chapt=0.
2. Ibid., chap. 5, http://www.nytimes.com/projects/2013/benghazi/#/?chapt=4.
3. Ibid., chap. 1.
4. Ibid.
5. Federal Research Division, Library of Congress, "Al-Qaida in Libya: A Profile" (Washington, D.C., August 2012), http://www.fas.org/irp/world/para/aq-libya-loc.pdf.
6. Michael R. Gordon, Eric Schmitt, and Michael S. Schmidt, with reporting from David D. Kirkpatrick and Suliman Ali Zway, "Libya Warnings Were Plentiful, but Unspecific," *New York Times* http://www.nytimes.com/2012/10/30/world/middleeast/no-specific-warnings-in-benghazi-attack.html?_r=1&, 1.
7. Ibid.
8. Ibid., 3.
9. Kirkpatrick, "A Deadly Mix in Benghazi," chap. 1.
10. The quotations that follow from this article are from David D. Kirkpatrick and Steven Lee Myers, "Libya Attack Brings Challenges for U.S.," September 12, 2012, mobile.nytimes.com/2012/09/13/world/middleeast/us-envoy-to-libya-is-reported-killed.html.
11. Ibid.
12. Eli Lake, "Benghazi's Al Qaeda Connection," *Daily Beast*, October 7, 2013, http://www.thedailybeast.com/articles/2013/10/07/benghazi-s-al-qaeda-connection.html.
13. U.S. Senate Select Committee on Intelligence, *Review of the Terrorist Attacks on U.S. Facilities in Benghazi, Libya, with Additional Views*, September 11–12, 2012. January 15, 2014, http://www.intelligence.senate.gov/benghazi2014/benghazi.pdf
14. US Department of State, "Unclassified" ARB Report, accessed February 26, 2014, http://www.state.gov/documents/organization/202446.pdf (hereinafter "ARB report"), 22.
15. Ibid.
16. Catherine Herridge, "Analysis of social media in Libya finds no reference to anti-Islam film on day of attack," Fox News, December 18, 2012, http://www.foxnews.com/politics/2012/12/18/no-reference-to-anti-islam-film-on-social-media-in-libya-day-attack-analysis/.
17. Kirkpatrick, "A Deadly Mix in Benghazi," chap. 4, http://www.nytimes.com/projects/2013/benghazi/#/?chapt=3.
18. ARB report, 15, 16.

19. Hadeel Al Shalchi, "In Libya, deadly fury took U.S. envoys by surprise," Reuters, September 12, 2012, http://mobile.reuters.com/article/idUSBRE88C02Q20120913?irpc=932.
20. Paul Schemm and Maggie Michael, "Libyan witnesses recount organized Benghazi attack," Associated Press, October 27, 2012, http://bigstory.ap.org/article/libyan-witnesses-recount-organized-benghazi-attack.
21. David Brock and Ari Rabin-Havt, *The Benghazi Hoax* (Media Matters for America, 2013), 64.
22. Ibid., 62
23. See the "About Crisis Group" section of the International Crisis Group website, which specifically champions the Responsibility to Protect doctrine, at http://www.crisisgroup.org/en/about.aspx. The doctrine was coauthored by Gareth Evans, the ICG's president emeritus, as further documented in my article "Obama's Benghazi investigator tied to Libya bombing," WND, November 3, 2012, http://www.wnd.com/2012/11/obamas-benghazi-investigator-tied-to-libya-bombing.
24. Brock and Rabin-Havt, *The Benghazi Hoax*, 53.
25. Ibid., 54.
26. "Statement on the Attacks on the US Facilities in Benghazi, Libya before the Senate Armed Services Committee as Delivered by Secretary of Defense Leon E. Panetta, Washington, D.C., Thursday, February 07, 2013," posted on the website of the U.S. Department of Defense, http://www.defense.gov/speeches/speech.aspx?speechid=1748.
27. U.S. House of Representatives, "Interim Progress Report for the Members of the House Republican Conference on the Events Surrounding the September 11, 2012 Terrorist Attacks in Benghazi, Libya," 19.
28. Brock and Rabin-Havt, *The Benghazi Hoax*, 33.
29. Ibid., 34.

10. FROM BENGHAZI TO . . . THE BOSTON BOMBING?

1. Mariam Karouny, "U.S.-trained Syrian rebels returning to fight: senior rebel source," Reuters, March 14, 2013, http://www.reuters.com/article/2013/03/14/us-syria-crisis-rebels-idUSBRE92D15E20130314.
2. David S. Cloud and Raja Abdulrahim, "Update: U.S. training Syrian rebels; White House 'stepped up assistance,'" *Los Angeles Times*, June 21, 2013, http://articles.latimes.com/2013/jun/21/world/la-fg-wn-cia-syria-20130621.
3. Aaron Klein, "Mideast war in March?" WND, February 24, 2012, http://www.wnd.com/2012/02/mideast-war-in-march/.
4. Aaron Klein, "Just lovely: Look who U.S. is helping now," WND, May 22, 2012, http://www.wnd.com/2012/05/just-lovely-look-who-u-s-is-helping-now.
5. Thomas Hegghammer, "Syrian's Foreign Fighters," *Foreign Policy* magazine, December 9, 2013, http://mideastafrica.foreignpolicy.com/posts/2013/12/09/syrias_foreign_fighters#sthash.A56j4wLb.EOpduFk.
6. Thomas Hegghammer, "Number of foreign fighters from Europe in Syria is historically unprecedented. Who should be worried?" *The Monkey Cage* (*Washington Post* blog), November 27, 2013, http://www.washingtonpost.com/blogs/monkey-cage/wp/2013/11/27/number-of-foreign-fighters-from-europe-in-syria-is-historically-unprecedented-who-should-be-worried/ ; and Sophie Cousins,

"Australian fighters in Syria alarm officials," Al Jazeera, February 4, 2014, http://www.aljazeera.com/indepth/features/2014/02/australian-fighters-syria-alarm-officials-201422132139299187.html.

7. Federal Research Division, Library of Congress, "Al-Qaida in Libya: A Profile" (Washington, D.C., August 2012), http://www.fas.org/irp/world/para/aq-libya-loc.pdf.
8. Steve Scherer, "Western countries alarmed as Libya slides towards chaos," Reuters, March 6, 2014, http://uk.reuters.com/article/2014/03/06/uk-libya-conference-idUKBREA2523B20140306.
9. Michelle Nichols, "Libya arms fueling conflicts in Syria, Mali and beyond: U.N. experts," Reuters, April 9, 2013, http://www.reuters.com/article/2013/04/09/us-libya-arms-un-idUSBRE93814Y20130409.
10. James Risen, Mark Mazzetti, and Michael S. Schmidt, "U.S.-Approved Arms for Libya Rebels Fell into Jihadis' Hands," *New York Times*, December 5, 2012, http://www.nytimes.com/2012/12/06/world/africa/weapons-sent-to-libyan-rebels-with-us-approval-fell-into-islamist-hands.html?pagewanted=all&_r=0.
11. Nichols, "Libya arms fueling conflicts in Syria, Mali and beyond."
12. Karl Vick, "Petraeus: Terrorists with Missiles Could Down Global Air Traffic," *Time* magazine, January 28, 2014, http://world.time.com/2014/01/28/petraeus-egypts-israel-militants-rockets/.
13. Aaron Klein, "U.S. facing al-Qaida payback strike?" WND, August 3, 2013, http://www.wnd.com/2013/08/u-s-facing-al-qaida-retaliation-strike/.
14. Adam Nossiter, "Some Algeria Attackers Are Placed at Benghazi," *New York Times*, January 23, 2013, http://www.nytimes.com/2013/01/23/world/africa/some-algeria-attackers-are-placed-at-benghazi.html?_r=0.
15. Paul Cruickshank et al., "Sources: 3 al Qaeda operatives took part in Benghazi attack," CNN, May 4, 2013, http://edition.cnn.com/2013/05/02/world/africa/us-libya-benghazi-suspects/index.html.
16. Mahmoud Habboush, with reporting by Ali Abdelatti, Reuters "Al Qaeda confirms death of bin Laden confidant Libi," *Chicago Tribune*, September 11, 2012, http://articles.chicagotribune.com/2012-09-11/news/sns-rt-us-security-qaedabre88a04l-20120910_1_libi-abu-yahya-zawahiri.
17. Cruickshank et al., "Sources: 3 al Qaeda operatives took part in Benghazi attack."
18. Ibid.
19. Liz Sly and Ahmed Ramadan, "Syrian extremists amputated a man's hand and live-tweeted it," *Washington Post*, February 28, 2014, http://www.washingtonpost.com/blogs/worldviews/wp/2014/02/28/syrian-extremists-amputated-a-mans-hand-and-live-tweeted-it/.
20. Daniel Wagner, "The Dark Side of the Free Syrian Army," *Huffington Post*, December 31, 2012, http://www.huffingtonpost.com/daniel-wagner/dark-side-free-syrian_b_2380399.html.
21. "ASIA/Syria—Abuse of the opposition forces, 'ethnic cleansing' of Christians in Homs, where Jesuits remains," *Agenzia Fides*, March 21, 2012, http://www.fides.org/aree/news/newsdet.php?idnews=31228&lan=eng.
22. Perry Chiaramonte, "Libya's lurch toward Shariah sends chill through Christian community," Fox News, January 12, 2014, http://www.foxnews.com/world/2014/01/12/libya-lurch-toward-shariah-sends-chill-through-christian-community/.

APPENDIX A: LIES AND MISLEADING CLAIMS

1. Amie Parnes, "Obama: Extremists used film 'as an excuse' to harm US interests," The Hill, September 20, 2012, http://thehill.com/homenews/administration/250813-obama-extremists-used-film-as-an-excuse-to-harm-us-interests.
2. Catherine Herridge, "Report sheds light on ex-CIA deputy director's role in Benghazi talking points," Fox News, February 4, 2014, http://www.foxnews.com/politics/2014/02/04/report-sheds-light-on-ex-cia-director-role-in-benghazi-talking-points/.
3. Robin Banerji, "Did Ansar al-Sharia carry out Libya attack?" BBC, September 12, 2012, http://www.bbc.com/news/world-africa-19575753.
4. Leila Fadel, "Consulate Attack Preplanned, Libya's President Says," NPR, September 16, 2012, http://www.npr.org/2012/09/16/161228170/consulate-attack-preplanned-libya-s-president-says.
5. Jake Tapper, "Ambassador Susan Rice: Libya Attack Not Premeditated," ABC News, September 16, 2012, http://abcnews.go.com/blogs/politics/2012/09/ambassador-susan-rice-libya-attack-not-premeditated/.
6. Aaron Klein, "Egypt's Morsi behind murder of U.S. ambassador?" WND, July 2, 2013, http://www.wnd.com/2013/07/egypts-morsi-behind-murder-of-u-s-ambassador/.
7. Warner Todd Huston, "CNN Ignores Real Goal of Cairo Riots: Freedom of Blind Sheik," Breitbart News, September 14, 2012, http://www.breitbart.com/Big-Journalism/2012/09/13/Cairo-Riots-Were-Not-Over-Offensive-American-Movie-Freedom-of-Blind-Sheik-The-Goal.
8. Statement from Senators Graham, McCain, and Ayotte 11/27/2012," Press Room (Senator Graham's official press release website), November 27, 2012, http://www.lgraham.senate.gov/public/index.cfm?FuseAction=PressRoom.PressReleases&ContentRecord_id=44354784-f8c9-664b-6178-c23a24d5c1ee&IsPrint=true.
9. U.S. House of Representatives, Interim Progress Report for the Members of the House Republican Conference on the Events Surrounding the September 11, 2012 Terrorist Attacks in Benghazi, Libya (April 23, 2013), https://goodlatte.house.gov/system/uploads/229/original/Libya-Progress-Report.pdf.
10. Ibid.
11. US Department of State, "Unclassified" ARB Report, accessed February 26, 2014, http://www.state.gov/documents/organization/202446.pdf. Hereinafter, "ARB report."
12. Aaron Klein, "Benghazi witnesses: Security 'not armed,' WND, November 23, 2013, http://www.wnd.com/2013/11/benghazi-witnesses-security-personnel-were-not-armed/
13. "VIDEO: Rep. Lynn Westmoreland on Benghazi eyewitness testimony," Fox News, November 26, 2013, http://video.foxnews.com/v/2871289782001/rep-lynn-westmoreland-on-benghazi-eyewitness-testimony/#sp=show-clips.
14. James Risen, Mark Mazzetti, and Michael S. Schmidtt, "U.S.-Approved Arms for Libya Rebels Fell into Jihadis' Hands," New York Times, December 6, 2012, http://www.nytimes.com/2012/12/06/world/africa/weapons-sent-to-libyan-rebels-with-us-approval-fell-into-islamist-hands.html?pagewanted=all&_r=0.
15. Michael R. Gordon and Mark Landler, "Backstage Glimpses of Clinton as Dogged Diplomat, Win or Lose," New York Times, February 2, 2013, http://www.nytimes.com/2013/02/03/us/politics/in-behind-scene-blows-and-triumphs-sense-of-clinton-future.htm.

16. Eli Lake, "CIA Contractor Testimony Could Undermine Obama on Benghazi," Daily Beast, November 6, 2013, http://www.thedailybeast.com/articles/2013/11/06/cia-contractor-testimony-could-undermine-obama-on-benghazi.html.
17. Larry Shaughnessy, "Military chief disputes 'stand down' claim on Benghazi," CNN, June 12, 2013, http://security.blogs.cnn.com/2013/06/12/military-chief-disputes-stand-down-claim-on-benghazi/.
18. ARB report, 23.
19. Aaron Klein, "Now CIA contradicts gov't Benghazi account," WND, December 16, 2013, http://www.wnd.com/2013/12/now-cia-contradicts-govt-benghazi-account/.
20. "TRANSCRIPTS Hillary Clinton Senate Hearing: Questions from Senators Flake, Coons, and McCain," CNN, January 23, 2013, http://transcripts.cnn.com/TRANSCRIPTS/1301/23/cnr.04.html.
21. United States House of Representatives Committee on Oversight and Government Reform, Benghazi Attacks: Investigative Update: Interim Report on the Accountability Review Board (September 16, 2013), http://oversight.house.gov/wp-content/uploads/2013/09/Report-for-Members-final.pdf.
22. Michael R. Gordon and Mark Landler, "Backstage Glimpses of Clinton as Dogged Diplomat, Win or Lose," New York Times, February 2, 2013, http://www.nytimes.com/2013/02/03/us/politics/in-behind-scene-blows-and-triumphs-sense-of-clinton-future.html?action=click&module=Search®ion=searchResults%230&version=&url=http%3A%2F%2Fquery.nytimes.com%2Fsearch%2Fsitesearch%2F%23%2FBackstage%2BGlimpses%2Bof%2BClinton%2Bas%2BDogged%2BDiplomat%2C%2BWin%2Bor%2BLose%2F.

APPENDIX B: QUESTIONS FOR THE HOUSE SELECT COMMITTEE ON BENGHAZI

1. U.S. Senate Select Committee on Intelligence, *Review of the Terrorist Attacks on U.S. Facilities in Benghazi, Libya, with Additional Views*, September 11–12, 2012 (January 15, 2014), http://www.intelligence.senate.gov/benghazi2014/benghazi.pdf, 39.
2. Leigh Ann Caldwell, "GOP Rep: Benghazi Not a 'Complete Cover-Up,'" New Day (CNN blog), November 18, 2013, http://newday.blogs.cnn.com/2013/11/18/rep-westmoreland-weighs-in-on-hearing-with-benghazi-eye-witnesses/.
3. US Department of State, "Unclassified" ARB Report, accessed February 26, 2014, http://www.state.gov/documents/organization/202446.pdf (hereinafter ARB report), 5.
4. ARB report, 21.
5. Jessica Donati, Ghaith Shennib, and Firas Bosalum, "The adventures of a Libyan weapons dealer in Syria," Reuters, June 18, 2013, http://www.reuters.com/article/2013/06/18/us-libya-syria-idUSBRE95H0WC20130618
6. C. J. Chivers and Eric Schmitt, "Arms Airlift to Syria Rebels Expands, with Aid from C.I.A.," *New York Times*, March 24, 2013, http://www.nytimes.com/2013/03/25/world/middleeast/arms-airlift-to-syrian-rebels-expands-withcia-aid.html?_r=0.
7. James Risen, Mark Mazzetti, and Michael S. Schmidt, "U.S.-Approved Arms for Libya Rebels Fell into Jihadis' Hands," *New York Times*, December 5, 2012, http://www.nytimes.com/2012/12/06/world/africa/weapons-sent-to-libyan-rebels-with-us-approvalfell-into-islamist-hands.html?pagewanted=all.

8. Catherine Herridge and Pamela Browne, "Was Syrian weapons shipment factor in ambassador's Benghazi visit?" Fox News, October 25, 2012, http://www.foxnews.com/politics/2012/10/25/was-syrian-weapons-shipment-factor-in-ambassadors-benghazi-visit/.
9. Jake Tapper, "Exclusive: Dozens of CIA operatives on the ground during Benghazi attack," *The Lead* (CNN blog), August 1, 2013, http://thelead.blogs.cnn.com/2013/08/01/exclusive-dozens-of-cia-operatives-on-the-ground-during-benghazi-attack.
10. Risen, Mazzetti, and Schmidt, "U.S.-Approved Arms for Libya Rebels Fell into Jihadis' Hands."
11. ARB report, 22–27.
12. Eli Lake, "CIA Contractor Testimony Could Undermine Obama on Benghazi," *Daily Beast*, November 6, 2013, http://www.thedailybeast.com/articles/2013/11/06/cia-contractor-testimony-could-undermine-obama-on-benghazi.html.
13. "Transcript: Whistle-blower's account of Sept. 11 Libya terror attack," Fox News, May 8, 2013, http://www.foxnews.com/politics/2013/05/08/transcript-whistle-blower-account-sept-11-libya-terror-attack/.
14. Aaron Klein, "Benghazi witnesses: Security 'not armed,' *WND Politics*, November 23, 2013, http://www.wnd.com/2013/11/benghazi-witnesses-security-personnel-were-not-armed/.
15. "VIDEO: Rep. Lynn Westmoreland on Benghazi eyewitness testimony," Fox News, November 26, 2013, http://video.foxnews.com/v/2871289782001/rep-lynn-westmoreland-on-benghazi-eyewitness-testimony/#sp=show-clips.
16. ARB report.
17. Aaron Klein, "Now CIA contradicts gov't Benghazi account," WND, December 16, 2013, http://www.wnd.com/2013/12/now-cia-contradicts-govt-benghazi-account/.
18. ARB report, 23.
19. Ibid., 26
20. Ibid.
21. Ibid., 27.
22. U.S. Senate Select Committee on Intelligence, *Review of the Terrorist Attacks on U.S. Facilities in Benghazi, Libya, with Additional Views*, 7–8.
23. Josh Rogin, "Exclusive: John McCain on His Meeting with the Muslim Brotherhood in Cairo," *Daily Beast*, August 6, 2013, http://www.thedailybeast.com/articles/2013/08/06/exclusive-john-mccain-on-his-meeting-with-the-muslim-brotherhood-in-cairo.html.
24. U.S. Senate Select Committee on Intelligence, *Review of the Terrorist Attacks on U.S. Facilities in Benghazi, Libya, with Additional Views*, "Additional Views of Vice Chairman Chambliss and Senators Burr, Risch, Coats, Rubio, and Coburn," 11.
25. Catherine Herridge, "Exclusive: Classified cable warned consulate couldn't withstand 'coordinated attack,'" Fox News, October 31, 2012, http://www.foxnews.com/politics/2012/10/31/exclusive-us-memo-warned-libya-consulate-couldnt-withstand-coordinated-attack/.
26. Michael R. Gordon and Mark Landler, "Backstage Glimpses of Clinton as Dogged Diplomat, Win or Lose," *New York Times*, February 2, 2013, http://www.nytimes.com/2013/02/03/us/politics/in-behind-scene-blows-and-triumphs-senseof-clinton-future.html?action=click&module=Search®ion=searchResul

ts%230&version=&url=http%3A%2F%2Fquery.nytimes.com%2Fsearch%2Fsitesearch%2F%23%2FBackstage%2BGlimpses%2Bof%2BClinton%2Bas%2BDogged%2BDiplomat%2C%2BWin%2Bor%2BLose%2F.

27. U.S. Senate Select Committee on Intelligence, *Review of the Terrorist Attacks on U.S. Facilities in Benghazi, Additional Views*, 11.
28. Stephen F. Hayes, "Lawmakers: CIA #2 Lied to Us about Benghazi," *Weekly Standard*, March 3, 2014, http://www.weeklystandard.com/blogs/lawmakers-cia-2-lied-us-about-benghazi_782724.html.
29. Catherine Herridge, "Report sheds light on ex-CIA deputy director's role in Benghazi talking points," Fox News Politics, February 4, 2014, http://www.foxnews.com/politics/2014/02/04/report-sheds-light-on-ex-cia-director-role-in-benghazi-talking-points/.

APPENDIX C: RESPONSE TO *HARD CHOICES* BY HILLARY CLINTON

1. Hillary Clinton, *Hard Choices,* (New York: Simon & Schuster, 2014), Kindle edition, chap. 17.
2. Clinton, *Hard Choices*, chap. 17.
3. Ibid.
4. Ibid.
5. "What They Said, Before and After the Attack in Libya," *New York Times*, September 12, 2012, http://www.nytimes.com/interactive/2012/09/12/us/politics/libya-statements.html?_r=0.
6. Clinton, *Hard Choices*, chap. 17.
7. Ibid.
8. Ibid.
9. "Transcript: Whistle-blower's account of Sept. 11 Libya terror attack," Fox News, May 8, 2013, http://www.foxnews.com/politics/2013/05/08/transcript-whistle-blower-account-sept-11-libya-terror-attack/.
10. Catherine Herridge, "Report sheds light on ex-CIA deputy director's role in Benghazi talking points," Fox News, February 4, 2014, http://www.foxnews.com/politics/2014/02/04/report-sheds-light-on-ex-cia-director-role-in-benghazi-talking-points/.
11. Clinton, *Hard Choices*, chap. 17.
12. Ibid., chap. 17.
13. Kimberly Dozier, "CIA Benghazi team clash led to 'stand down' report," Associated Press, December 14, 2013, http://bigstory.ap.org/article/cia-benghazi-team-clash-led-stand-down-report.
14. Clinton, *Hard Choices*, chap. 17.
15. Eli Lake, "CIA Contractor Testimony Could Undermine Obama on Benghazi," Daily Beast, November 6, 2013, http://www.thedailybeast.com/articles/2013/11/06/cia-contractor-testimony-could-undermine-obama-on-benghazi.html.
16. Clinton, *Hard Choices*, chap. 17.
17. Senate Select Committee on Intelligence "Review of the terrorist attacks on U.S. Facilities in Benghazi, Libya;" January 15, 2014 http://www.fas.org/irp/congress/2014_rpt/benghazi.pdf.
18. Clinton, *Hard Choices*, chap. 17.

19. Senate Select Committee on Intelligence "Review of the terrorist attacks on U.S. Facilities in Benghazi, Libya;"
20. Clinton, *Hard Choices*, chap. 17.
21. Ibid.
22. United States House of Representatives Committee on Oversight and Government Reform, "Benghazi Attacks: Investigative Update: Interim Report on the Accountability Review Board" (September 16, 2013), http://oversight.house.gov/wp-content/uploads/2013/09/Report-for-Members-final.pdf,
23. Full text, Majority Staff Report, House Foreign Affairs Committee, "Benghazi: Where is the State Department Accountability?" Available at http://foreignaffairs.house.gov/sites/republicans.foreignaffairs.house.gov/files/HFAC%20Majority%20Staff%20Report%20on%20Benghazi.pdf.
24. Clinton, *Hard Choices*, chap. 17.
25. Ibid.

INDEX

Y

Z

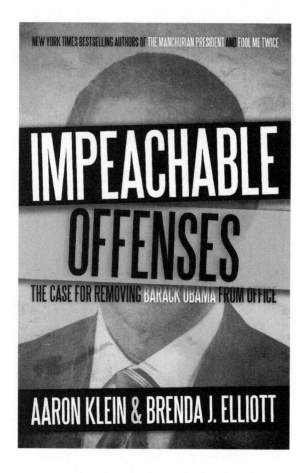

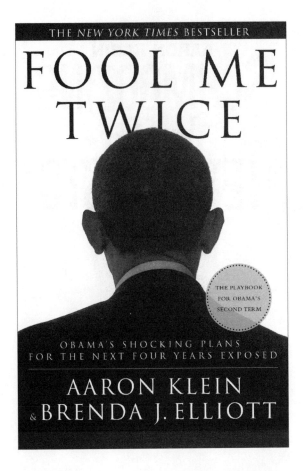

PRESENTS

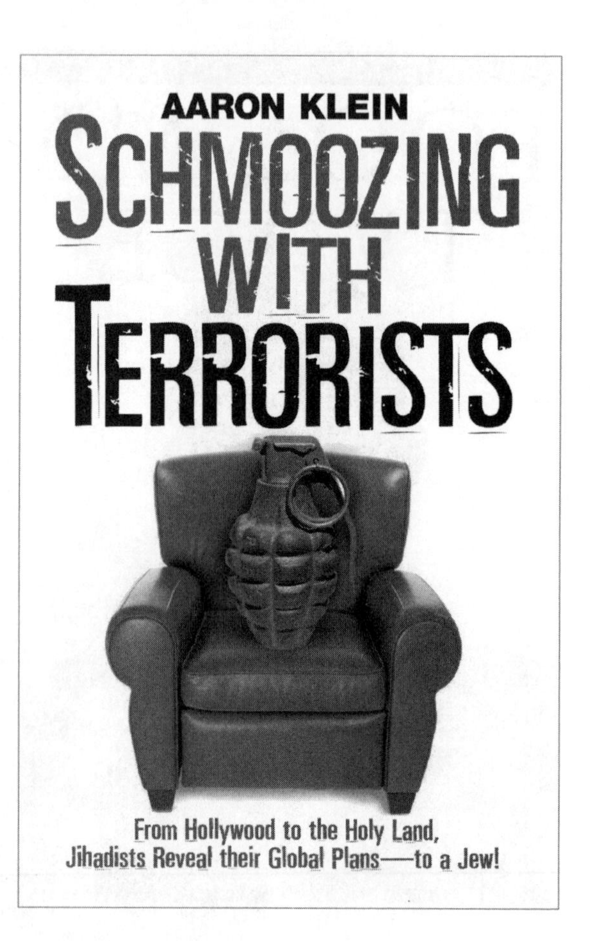

In a time of unprecedented danger for the West, it's crucial that Americans understand the true nature of the adversaries we face and how we are making them bolder each day. Join Aaron Klein, award-winning journalist and radio commentator, as he schmoozes and kvetches with radical clerics, suicide bombers, the parents of potential child martyrs and the leaders of the world's most dangerous terrorist organizations.

WND Books • A WND COMPANY • WASHINGTON DC • WNDBOOKS.COM

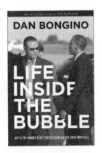

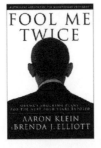

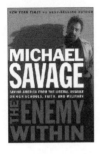

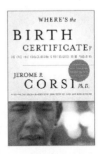

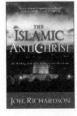

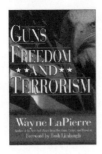

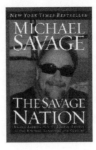